Writing and Reading to Learn

Writing and Reading to Learn

edited by

Nea Stewart-Dore

Primary English Teaching Association

The views expressed in this publication are not necessarily those of the Board or members of the Primary English Teaching Association.

ISBN 0 909955 65 4
Dewey 372.6044
First published November 1986
Reprinted April 1987
Copyright © Primary English Teaching Association 1986
PO Box 167 Rozelle NSW 2039 Australia
Design consultant: Mark Jackson
Cover photograph: courtesy of the Principal, Bletchington Public School, Orange, and Resource Services, NSW Dept of Education
Typeset in 10/11 Souvenir and printed by
Bridge Printery Pty Ltd
29-35 Dunning Avenue Rosebery NSW 2018

Foreword

Three-year-old Andrew suddenly interrupted the story I was reading him—'That's A for Andrew!'

His interest fired, he unsnuggled himself, wriggled off my lap, searched for and found his 'magic slate', and ordered me to copy the A he had noticed on the page.

'Now write down how *your* name begins,' he directed, first me, and then each of the others in the room. When I pointed out that we had written 'letters' on his slate, he repeated the word with interest and then excitedly drew my attention to the fact that my name and his sister Jennica's 'begin the same.'

Andrew is rapidly learning to become literate. Further, through countless brief incidents such as this, which bring together reading, writing and discussion, he is progressively shaping and refining his own reality and adding to his burgeoning knowledge base.

Writing and Reading to Learn urges teachers to think about what it means for children to learn to become literate in a variety of contexts. It raises the question of what we need to know about language, literacy and learning in order to help them become, and continue to develop as, confident, reflective, independent learners both in and out of school. It challenges us to examine and justify, or change,

- our literacy teaching practices
- the literary products we value
- the literacy learning experiences we provide for children

across curriculum boundaries throughout the years of primary schooling.

Throughout, the authors argue that we do children a disservice if we confine literacy teaching and learning to the Language Arts curriculum. Similarly, we do them a disservice if teaching practice is oriented towards the learning of content rather than towards the development of thinking and understanding. Maintaining that reading and writing are integral to learning to make sense of the world, they suggest that effective literacy teaching and learning strategies might foster that elusive but much-desired objective of 'thinking'.

This is a challenging book. It sets out to bridge the gap between current research and theory about literacy learning and teaching and teacher knowledge of that theory and research. Even more importantly, it addresses the possibly wider gap between what many teachers know and what they actually do in their classrooms. But it is not a recipe book. It does not attempt to provide handy hints or prescriptions for teaching which then become ritualized and little better than 'skill and drill' exercises.

It recognizes and acknowledges that change lies in teachers' hands. Provided they develop a sound rationale (derived from theory and research, as well as from demonstrably effective practice), teachers can and *do* generate worthwhile strategies for themselves.

The ideas in this book will help teachers develop that rationale. It provides practical theory and research information which extend our views on literacy and learning.

Emphasizing the significance of context and purpose in reading and writing, it establishes some parameters for action by providing teachers with starting points for considering how writing and reading are related in their classrooms. It proposes that one way of achieving excellence is through a review of our practices in the light of
- careful observation of children using written language
- critical appraisal of the texts and tasks we employ.

Although challenging, Writing and Reading to Learn is an exciting book. Read thoughtfully, and referred to often, it could provide teachers with a tool to change the way they 'read and write the [school] world'.

John Dwyer
Regional Director of Education
Brisbane South Region
Queensland Department of Education

Contents

Foreword John Dwyer	v
1 Literacy, Learning and Teaching Nea Stewart-Dore	1
2 Learning to be Literate—Naturally Brenda Parkes	9
3 Learning to Mean in Writing Frances Christie	21
4 Connecting Writing and Reading Michèle Anstey	35
5 Thinking-through Text Bert Morris	53
6 Writing and Reading to Learn Together Jan Weis with Nea Stewart-Dore	67

7 Writing and Reading Culturally
    Nea Stewart-Dore with Rosemary Guttormsen
    and Nicki Kennedy
	81

References	95
Index	99

Acknowledgements

For their generous contributions to this publication, I am indebted to:

the authors, for their collegiality, patience and thoughtful challenges;

John Dwyer, for his commitment to literacy, learning and teaching, and for penning the Foreword;

Phil. Cullen, Director of Primary Schools, and Merle O'Donovan, Inspector of Schools, Queensland Department of Education, for their guidance and encouragement;

David Boston, Judy George, Ian Weir, June Fox, Ross Zerk, Jan Weis and teachers and students of Capalaba, MacGregor and Sunnybank State Primary Schools for their willingness to share teaching practices;

Anne Russell, Brisbane College of Advanced Education, for her interest and photography;

Gay Harvey, for cheerful typing and revision of many drafts;

my Brisbane family, especially Colin, for their sacrifice of time.

Nea Stewart-Dore
Brisbane
September 1986

1 Literacy, Learning and Teaching

Nea Stewart-Dore
Brisbane College of Advanced Education

'What do I think I *do* when I write?' Twelve-year-old Mark could hardly believe the question was seriously intended. While drafting a play script to support group investigation of social relationships between miners and administrators on the Victorian goldfields in the 1850s, he signalled his need to break from his composing task. His teacher took the opportunity to probe his understanding of writing. This is his tape-recorded response.

'Gee, um I dunno. . . . I never thought about that . . . (*pause*) . . . um let me think . . . (*long pause—pencil twiddling, re-reading of draft and occasional sighing*) . . . Well (*deep breath*) I try, I try to um, get ideas down you know? Yeh, I get ideas down, like I think um on paper . . . what's, what's in my head . . . that's um the hard part 'coz I know what I mean to say, well most times anyway but uh, uh saying it, well . . . (*pause*) sometimes, um a lot of times it sort of . . . doesn't come out right, doesn't come out how I want, what it should be and uh . . . (*pause*) well you know, if somebody's gunna read it okay? If somebody's gunna read it, like you read this, I gotta make . . . (*pause*) make, um, make my meaning yours . . . yeh, I mean you have to know what I mean don't you if you're gunna read it? That's um hard to do, to do that 'coz I read . . . yeh, I read and I uh (*laughs*) I scratch out, make a mess you know? Scrumple up paper and cross all over (*pushing draft across the table*) . . . see? It's a *big* mess, a big mess, all those words changed I'll probably throw it away . . . like when I'm reading it over to write some more and I think that's not right so I scratch out like I gotta read and think at the same time . . . (*pause; looks up, grinning*). Yeh, I gotta read and think and um write all in together . . . (*pause*). That's pretty neat, eh?

'Freed' from having to guess an expected answer, and confident in the knowledge that his teacher *expects* him to explore his thinking, Mark constructs personal meaning and knowledge about how writing is linked with reading and thinking, to learn. His pleasure in making these connections and realizing new understandings is demonstrated by his postscript: 'That's pretty neat, eh?'

We too need to 'free' ourselves, especially from persistent tenets about literacy, its teaching and learning, so that we may explore, like Mark, what it *means* to *learn* to be literate.

This text aims to help you explore what it means to learn to be literate: to make meaning and create knowledge through written language in a variety of contexts in and out of school. It deals with children's early social transactions with print; with the kinds of understandings we need to reflect on and share professionally so that we may improve the *quality* of learning how to interpret the world through writing and reading; with relationships between writing (composing) and reading (comprehending); with texts that children write and read, and with how we might view those texts and plan to teach using them.

In pursuit of literate excellence

Just as we want to succeed at teaching, so we want children to learn successfully. Our task is to socialize children into reading and writing for varied purposes so that they can learn to think and to shape and extend their knowledge of language and of the world. In doing so, we have three options from which to choose.

1. We can choose to *preserve* the status quo. This means shunning innovation and change and clinging to what we think is the sanctity of 'tried and true' methods.

2. We can choose to *react* to numerous public pressures to go 'back to basics'. This means modifying our teaching/learning programs so that they satisfy demands that 'skills' be drilled, in isolation from each other and out of the context of their purposeful use.

3. We can choose to *create* opportunities to improve literacy teaching and learning. This means becoming keen observers of children and interacting with them as they work with written texts of various kinds.

The rationale for choosing the latter option, which this text supports, is to be found in a synthesis of three sources of information: recommendations for improvements in teaching and learning; theory and research findings; and what we gather ourselves as we investigate in our classrooms how children learn to be literate and to use literacy to understand their world.

1. Recommendations for improvement in teaching and learning

Two imperatives underpin and thematically link several Commonwealth government documents released since 1980. These recommend improvements be made in teaching and learning. The imperatives are:

(a) to review our teaching methods in the light of
the need for higher levels of attainment by all students ... ; the demand for coverage of new areas of knowledge and skill; and the need to respond to research evidence about how children learn (Q.E.R.C. 1985, p. 49)

(b) to focus on improving writing and reading achievement so that all students, having confidence in their reasoning ability, may become independent learners able not only to use appropriate text books but also to collect and order information and ideas, and structure them into coherent presentation (C.S.C. 1980, p. 20).

The Schools Commission (1984, p. 14) recommends we adopt teaching approaches which encourage

> curiosity, imagination and rationality, using discussion and reflection to enlarge understanding, reducing the amount of passive listening and a too-great emphasis on rote-learning and stressing the gathering and evaluation of information in solving problems.

Although these recommendations refer to practice in secondary schools, the primary school's role in laying the foundation for such ventures is prized. Without doubt, there is the intention that partnerships be formed between teachers *at different levels of schooling* to ensure that children will acquire

> a general capacity for learning skills rather than any particular learned skills. New skills will be constantly required ... all ... need to be able to communicate effectively in a wide range of public and private contexts (C.S.C. 1984, pp. 18-19).

To *preserve* the status quo in literacy teaching will deny children opportunities to extend their capacities to make meaning. As an editorial in *The Age* (2/5/85) argued:

> The question is not whether present levels of competence in English are declining or marginally improving, but whether they are adequate. . . . They are not.

To *react* to pressures which demand skills be drilled places us in the invidious position of having to defend to colleagues and parents why children find independent and original thought difficult, and why they may lack confidence in their capacity to communicate in new situations.

However, to pursue literate excellence—by integrating writing, reading, thinking and learning processes—we must challenge our assumptions about the processes and products of learning and about our practices of teaching. We must reflect about the meaning of learning to be literate. Above all, we must *create* a personal need to learn more about the nature, purposes and forms of literacy, so that our choice of teaching approach is well informed. We can do this by investigating further what it means to become literate in all subject areas. Such investigation is the subject of the remainder of this book.

2. *Theory and research findings*

(a) *Language learning processes*

Traditionally, development in written language has been seen as progression through a set of relatively discrete stages, classified and labelled to identify learning sequences. Even today, much literacy teaching rests on the assumption that definable sub-skills exist, and that children must learn these in order to progress to 'the next stage' of reading or writing growth.

Yet language is not learned in discrete chunks. Even though young children do not speak, write or read as adults do, they experience and use language in the same, purposeful ways. They experience, learn and use language in the total context of its use—to get things done, to express feelings, opinions and ideas, to imagine, to relate experience and so on. Parkes and Christie, in Chapters 2 and 3 respectively, provide specific instances of these language experiences, learnings and uses, especially in the early years.

What is especially important to acknowledge is that throughout life we all are constantly learning language, learning about language and learning through language.

As we live (and teach), so we meet fresh demands for language use. We learn to do new things with it—to conduct parent interviews, to persuade the Principal to our point of view or to formulate requests for transfer. We learn as well to do 'old' things better—to develop our storytelling skills, to revise and edit our teaching programs, or to explain to children what is involved in a task. If we pause to think for a moment, there are many, many instances of learning to do new things and to do 'old' things better with language, both within and beyond our teaching experience.

Like spoken language, written language learning is a developmental process, continually undergoing refinement. This occurs as we gather relevant information on which to draw, so that we may write and read more effectively for different purposes. To become effective written language users requires that we experience relevant text models of different kinds in sustained interaction with others.

Results of survey studies of how teachers actually go about 'teaching' reading and writing are, however, disturbing. Durkin (1978) discovered that teachers were more likely to test reading comprehension than teach it, while Lunzer and Gardner (1979) found that students were given little opportunity to reflect on their reading or to do more than 'short-burst' reading in class. Studies conducted by Applebee (1980; 1984) and his colleagues show that in secondary schools at least, students rarely produce extended writing. This is because teachers across the curriculum assign perfunctory tasks requiring only 'fill-in-the-gap' or restricted written responses. We need to review *our* practices to determine whether or not a similar situation obtains in our primary context.

Whatever the case, we need to rationalize and systematize our literacy teaching approaches. We must maintain balance, so that a focus on *process* does not blind us to the need to value equally the *products* of various teaching and learning strategies. To achieve this, we must undertake research inquiry in our own classrooms and explore what it means to become literate *there*.

To help us do this, Parkes' chapter outlines those aspects of 'kidwatching' necessary for observing children as interactive language users and for monitoring how they use language to make sense of their world. Other authors probe aspects of the implications of sharing text for published research and our own. In doing so, they heighten our sensitivity to the excitement and complexity of becoming literate. Throughout, the message is clear: as teachers, we must continue to learn about the nature and uses of literacy, as well as about text itself and how we can assist children to compose literate products.

(b) *The nature and features of text*

The nature and features of text can be examined from different perspectives. Concerned that the impact of recent enthusiasm for process approaches to writing teaching has emphasized 'process' to the exclusion of 'product' in text composition, Christie in Chapter 3 argues that we need to be able to recognize and analyse a range of written text types or genres if we are to guide children in the linguistic choices available to them in making meaning through writing. This involves understanding how language varies according to use, and how we organize knowledge and ideas differently to serve different purposes. Christie explains these variations by examining samples of children's writing, providing a compelling rationale for using relevant, 'good' models of different types of writing, or genres, in classrooms.

Any discussion of how text is organized must deal with cohesion, or how text 'hangs together' to integrate meaning and to help readers comprehend. Cohesion has to do (among other things) with those features of written text which link ideas and establish how they are related. Cohesion enables us to carry meaning forward as we read and to keep track of how information is tied together. Aspects of cohesion are crucial to Christie's descriptions of children's writing.

While their findings are not explored in detail here, reading researchers too have examined the importance of cohesion. For a gentle introduction to cohesion and how it contributes to the integration of meaning when reading text, teachers might consult a special issue of the *Australian Journal of Reading* (6, 1, March 1983).

Research into how students might be taught about text organization to better understand and retell what they have read was begun by Meyer (1975). She identified how ideas may be arranged to signal their importance and their relationship to each other in written text. She found that there were several kinds of recurring patterns in informational or expository text—patterns of listing, cause-effect, problem-solution, comparison-contrast, and description or elaboration. These patterns she labelled 'top-level structure', since in well-written text they are signalled early on, at the 'top-level', where important ideas precede less significant detail 'lower down' in the text. From these and other findings, top-level structure has been investigated for 'its potential in learning from text' (Bartlett 1985, p. 220).

Such research directs attention to expository text itself, and how as readers we may make sense of it. It thus focuses principally on reading. Writing is regarded as *recalled* response to reading. It does, however, introduce teachers to the idea of learning *from* text. Considering this, Morris in Chapter 5 examines how teachers might view informational text in primary classrooms. He provides background to the movement in the 1970s towards what became termed 'Content Area Reading' in an effort to distinguish the purposes for reading in classrooms. In some ways this label artificially separates learning to read from reading to learn, yet it does draw attention to differences in how we structure knowledge through written language. It is this latter theme that Morris pursues, along with reading purposes, by outlining methods for helping children to read strategically and thoughtfully.

Further consideration is given to helping children understand the nature and structure of text in Weis and Stewart-Dore's account in Chapter 6 of action-research conducted in a Year 7 class (the final year of primary schooling in Queensland). Here the authors report on attempts to fuse reading and writing teaching using a modification of the Effective Reading in Content Areas (ERICA) model, developed by Morris and Stewart-Dore (1984). The major objective was to demonstrate how children's text processing strategies used in Language Arts and Library 'reading' sessions might be applied to situations in other curriculum areas (such as Maths, Social Studies, Art, Science and Health) which demanded reflective thinking, and comprehension and composition of meanings. After an analysis of language and thinking curriculum objectives, a series of interrelated activities requiring children to reflect on and debate text meaning was devised. These activities supported learning through reading, writing and small group discussion.

(c) *Relationships between comprehending and composing*

There is much speculation about how reading and writing are related. One theory, (Tierney and Pearson 1983), suggests that both reading and writing are 'acts of composing'. Thus:

> From a reader's perspective, meaning is created as a reader uses his background experience together with the author's cues to come to grips with what the writer is getting him to do or think *and* what the reader decides and creates for himself.
> (p. 33)

According to this view, a reader simultaneously perceives an author's intended meaning and determines a goal for reading. (Why am I reading this? What do I want to do as a result?) While reading a text, the reader may modify such goals, taking up different stances as 'critic, co-author, editor, character, reporter, eye-witness, etc.' The reader does this by drawing on previous knowledge and experience (and what it is thought the author intends) to create an integrated, complete textual meaning. Anstey in Chapter 4 explores how this might happen, using a narrative text as an example.

Believing that writing and reading serve to integrate learning in all curriculum areas and that children do not separate language from learning, Anstey provides a framework for planning a literacy program in the middle years of primary schooling. The curriculum implications of what she says address Squire's (1983, p. 25) proposition that:

> because language learning and language processing involve cognitive processes basic to every discipline, application to the discipline is critical if children are to learn to think in the discipline.

Our failure to recognize this has unfortunately led to practices which don't necessarily enable children to learn strategies appropriate for making meaning from and through text. This failure, according to Squire (1983, p. 23),

> impedes our efforts not only to teach children to read and write, but also our efforts to teach them to think.

(d) Writing and reading: thinking and learning

Although the precise nature of how writing and reading are related has yet to be established, it is generally agreed that both are thinking processes. If we accept that language and thinking are interdependent, then we can assume that they facilitate each other to promote learning. Flower and Hayes (1980) remind us that when we write, we review our knowledge, actively apply our understanding, analyse and synthesize what we mean, and constantly evaluate the text we are composing as we move back and forth to create meaning for ourselves and others.

As recursive back-and-forth thinking processes, reading and writing require that we regress in order to progress. Mark, quoted at the beginning of this chapter, gives testimony to this active meaning-making process. He demonstrates how writing and reading involve complex interactions between meaning-maker and text, as he strives to solve the problem of how to 'make my meaning yours'. The common task for both writer and reader is to work through meaning intentions using various sources of information available to both: intention and purpose; prior knowledge of content, language and relevant language-thinking strategies; and the features of written text.

In classroom situations, we ask children to respond in writing to knowledge and experience, especially that gained from reading. In doing so, we need to ensure that children are shown how to use their thinking capacities to reflect, infer, hypothesize, generalize and conclude, so that their understandings of the world and how language works can be extended. Such action reinforces what they have been doing successfully in all language and learning situations since birth—culling from the plethora of information in their environment that which serves their *intention* to make sense of their world. But reinforcement is not enough.

From Armbruster and Brown's (1984) research comes the suggestion that we should also teach children how to *control* their learning from and through text by teaching them how to plan, monitor and evaluate the understandings they create of experience—in our instance, experience of school subject matter. Thus the dimension of metacognition needs to be taken into account as we promote children's interaction with text and mind. Metacognition refers to 'knowing what you know' and 'how you know', developed by reflecting on your very thinking processes. This is something that Mark was able to do so well in his response to the question 'What do you think you do when you write?' Such attention would certainly do away with multiple choice/one-word/restricted length responses to questions about text which do not engage children's curiosity, yet are frequently posed by us.

Several authors in this text address how we might engage children's language-thinking capacities to learn through writing and reading. The notion of linguistic choice that Christie refers to in Chapter 3 is prime among the ideas we must consider if we are to help children write well-composed products. Reference has already been made to Anstey's consideration of the reciprocal processes of writing and reading, while Morris outlines some of the kinds of thinking necessary to extract information from text. Weis and Stewart-Dore explain in Chapter 6 how children's thinking can be enhanced through a focused process approach to developing concepts in Social Studies, and, finally, Chapter 7 synthesizes how language and thinking are engaged when cultural artefacts such as computers and newspapers are used.

In each case, the authors imply, where they do not make explicit, the close relationship between language and cognitive growth. The ideas presented are intended to prompt teachers to reconsider the role that thinking plays in learning through language, and to dissuade them from separating the language modes from learning to reason in the various school subject disciplines.

3. *Investigating literacy and learning in our classrooms*

Teacher educators and curriculum developers have long recommended action research as an avenue for teachers to explore aspects of teaching and learning in their classrooms. If we are to extend our personal knowledge of how children learn to become literate, we need to investigate how they approach various language learning tasks in our classrooms. While every teacher is obliged to monitor and report on the individual progress of children, this is frequently done only to 'assess' performance on discrete 'skills'. There are other reasons, however, for maintaining records of various kinds. Among these reasons are those of collecting appropriate data to:

(a) describe children's text composition and comprehension strategies
(b) monitor growth over time in various language-using capacities
(c) record how children perceive writing and reading tasks
(d) analyse what text features appear in children's writing as a base from which to plan instruction
(e) maintain a check on the variety of texts used in reading and writing instruction
(f) pinpoint where we need to refine our instructional support procedures
(g) record our personal growth and understanding of process strategies and their relationship to the production of literate outcomes.

Such record keeping not only permits us to report on children's language growth, but also provides information on which to reflect and from which to create new understandings of what it means to become literate.

Several chapters treat monitoring explicitly from different perspectives. Parkes recommends procedures for sharpening our observation skills of literacy learning in natural contexts. In Chapter 4, Anstey focuses our attention on evaluating not only knowledge of subject matter concepts, but also that relating to the nature of different texts which shape that knowledge. Morris, in Chapter 5, highlights the need to help students understand *how* they learn through text, thereby reinforcing our need to monitor their progress in doing so. The underlying principles of monitoring are further explored in Chapter 6, where Weis presents an account of having systematically observed and monitored teaching procedures to fuse writing and reading in Social Studies. By implication, the maintenance of 'field notes' is recommended, so that individual teachers may learn to analyse their practice and modify it in the light of discoveries they make in the process.

Although much literacy learning and teaching occurs in the context of classrooms, we must also acknowledge the many opportunities children have for learning to be literate beyond the classroom. We should study these extended contexts and be alert to their potential for moderating learning through writing and reading.

Thus, Parkes notes the impact of environmental print, while Stewart-Dore, Guttormsen and Kennedy examine in Chapter 7 the potential for extending children's literacy by using computers and newspapers. Naturally, there are other sources of and tools for 'learning to read and write the world' as well: television, commercial advertising, film, magazines, radio, and so on.

To employ such artefacts successfully as agents for language and cognitive growth demands enquiring minds. Teachers are uniquely placed, not only to extend learnings, but also, sadly, to stifle them. Only as we open our minds to the possibilities for exploring the world of comprehending and composing for ourselves will we be able to appreciate what it means to become literate—both socially and culturally.

Conclusion

This text brings together numerous threads that run through contemporary literacy learning and teaching theory, research and practice. It does not provide a recipe book of strategies for immediate adoption. Rather, it provokes thought about issues and methods. It demands that you draw on *your* knowledge and *your* practice to reflect on what you understand it means to learn to be literate and to learn through writing and reading.

Its arrangement is intended to map aspects of development through the pre-school and primary years. Overlap across chapters reinforces the idea that as we learn language and use it in different contexts for varying purposes and effects, we are continually practising language and thinking strategies already learned in order to refine and extend them.

Ultimately, the effect of the ideas presented rests with you, as you draw on your prior knowledge and experience to synthesize, infer and draw conclusions. It is my view, however, that change rests in your hands. Given your responsibility to enhance opportunities for literacy learning and to pursue literate excellence, I urge a *creative* response to the rest of this text.

2 Learning to be Literate—Naturally

Brenda Parkes
Brisbane College of Advanced Education

Children are born into a social community in which talk is a crucial aspect of their experience. Talk surrounds them from the moment they are born. They hear people talking to them, about them, and to others, and they hear talk from the TV, radio and other media. Through being immersed in the talk that accompanies the daily routines of their family, they begin to build up a system of meanings. As they are cuddled, fed, bathed, dressed, taken out, put to bed and so on, they continually hear talk, ranging through monologue, dialogue, song or nursery rhyme, depending on the language that each family uses in carrying out these tasks. Gradually, as routines are established in which children can anticipate what may happen next, they begin to initiate communication with adults. Naturally the adults respond, and so language develops.

Through shared daily living experiences children learn a system for making and sharing meaning. The contexts in which the experiences occur; the trust in those who share them; the opportunity to revisit experiences again and again, sometimes with the same and sometimes with different participants; the responsiveness of these participants—all help to nurture children's developing understanding of the intended meanings of the behaviours, experiences and interactions which make up their world. Although children's language experiences will vary considerably according to their circumstances, the learning of a system of meaning through social interaction is common to all.

Sarah, at 14 months, has a repertoire of 'bubbubbub', 'dadadad', 'mumum' for interacting with appropriate, and sometimes inappropriate people, and an ubiquitous 'uh' for anything which she notices and wishes to comment upon. She also has a range of strung together sounds of language, virtually a melody without the lyrics, through which she communicates her needs to her caregivers.

No one doubts for a moment that Sarah is a language user, or that eventually, through much experience in many kinds of varied situations, she will move toward mastery of the conventional spoken language model of her culture. No one sets out deliberately to 'teach' Sarah to talk, but all who interact with her realise that the best possible way for her to acquire language is to include her as a language user in whatever is going on in her family.

In a typical situation, Sarah's father is carrying her for a few minutes, and Sarah is taking the opportunity to scrutinize some of the objects in her environment that are literally well above her head.

'Uh,' she says, pointing to a toy on a shelf, 'Oleyolebubbub.'

'That's a dog,' says her father. 'That's Nanna's Footrot Flats Dog. Do you want to hold him?'

He hands the dog to Sarah, who cuddles it, making occasional noises. She examines it carefully, feeling the fur, poking her fingers at the eyes, keeping up a running burble as she goes. At this point she sets out to share what she is doing with her father again.

'Uh,' she says, pointing to the dog's foot, 'Uh.'

'That's the dog's foot,' says her father. Then, pointing to her foot, 'That's your foot, Sarah.'

Sarah looks at him and cuddles the dog again. Tiring of the dog, she points to her cup.

'Uh,' she says.

'Do you want a drink?' says her father.

'Uh,' Sarah responds much more urgently.

Father gets her cup and puts a little water in it. He hands it to Sarah.

'Ta Sarah,' he says, 'Here's your drink.' Sarah responds with something resembling 'ta' and drinks the water.

'Time for lunch now, Sarah,' says her mother. 'Come and I'll put you in your high chair.' She lifts Sarah in—'Up you go. Watch your foot. That's Sarah's foot,' as she lowers her into the chair.

'Here's your sandwiches. They're vegie sandwiches.'

Sarah picks up a sandwich and tries to feed her mother. 'Uh.'

'No, Sarah. They're your sandwiches. . . . Eat them up, that's a good girl. . . .'

These few minutes of conversation constitute some of the hundreds of language encounters that presently form an important part of Sarah's life with her family. She is their first baby, and so everyone is learning together about language learning. As Sarah employs her sounds of language with the intention of making meaning, the young parents observe and respond to her efforts and initiate further opportunities for learning.

Learning language

Cambourne (1984) has identified a number of conditions which contribute toward children becoming successful language users. These conditions are clearly evident as we watch Sarah grow into wider language use in varied contexts.

- She is constantly *immersed* in language as her family go about the business of living. The family routines—the shopping, visiting, eating, washing, gardening, playing and so on—are all rich in language learning experiences. Sometimes Sarah is a central figure in the situation; sometimes she plays a minor role, and sometimes she is an observer, but she is *always* a language learner through her involvement in the situation.

- Language is *demonstrated* to her, varying with whatever language form and function is appropriate to the particular situations she is sharing.

- There is *every expectation* from anyone she encounters that she will become a successful language user, and she is always included in situations as a purposeful language user.
- She takes *responsibility* for her own learning, initiating language encounters, exploring the objects and events in her world, and responding to the overtures of others.
- Her *approximations* to the adult model of spoken language are not only accepted, but are applauded and encouraged.
- Throughout her day there are countless opportunities for the *employment* of language: new things to 'uh' at and old ones to revisit and to expand on.
- In response to her efforts she receives *feedback*, both overt and subtle, unconditionally as the people in her world respond through language to her overtures and initiate others.

The acceptance and encouragement that she receives give her the security to be a 'risk taker' with language, to 'have a go', and the varied experiences she shares signal to her why and how people use language. In her own time, by interacting with language and the people, objects, events, behaviours, attitudes and feelings that make up her world, Sarah will work out how language is organized and used. She will achieve this by actively taking part in situations in which language serves genuine purposes. By the time she enters school she will be a competent language user without ever having been 'taught' in any formal sense. She will have learned crucial concepts about language, its nature and functions. For example, she will know that language is:

- structured systematically
- a way of making and expressing her meanings, of sharing her ideas and experiences with others
- functional, in that it can be used to find out about things and get things done.

In four or five short years, this is an impressive amount of learning.

How written language is learned

Learning written language need not be different from learning oral language. Children have demonstrated through their acquisition of oral language that they are very able learners, and parents and caregivers have demonstrated their capacity to initiate, respond to and nurture that learning. Given the same conditions, children can learn about written language first in partnership with their families, and later in partnerships between parents, teachers and other learners.

A number of recent studies (Harste, Burke and Woodward 1981; Goodman 1981) support the view that written language learning is an interactive process, and that by being part of a literate society with the opportunity to encounter written language in a variety of forms, children will learn to write and to read through engaging in writing and reading events.

Children will learn to organize the print in their environment just as they learn to organize the rest of their world. The studies mentioned above inform us of how children learn about written language before beginning school, and there is a growing body of evidence to show that young children know a great deal more about written language than we had previously thought. For example, the research report, 'Children, their language and world' (Harste, Burke and Woodward 1981), opens thus:

> We began our study of what 3, 4, 5, and 6 year old children know about language with a great deal of optimism, assured that they know much more about

print than what teachers and beginning reading and writing programs assume. What the results of our efforts have taught us is that we began not being optimistic enough; that children know much more than we or past researchers have ever dared to assume, and that many of the premises and assumptions with which we began must give way to a more generous perspective.

The nature of young children's knowledge about print has been discussed by Yetta Goodman (1981). She identified three major groups of principles that young children learn about written language as they interact with print. These are:

- functional principles, which include the understandings that children have about the reasons and purposes for written language
- semiotic principles, which are the understandings that children have about the ways that meaning is represented through written language
- linguistic principles, which are understandings about orthographic and graphophonic systems.

Children in a literate society start learning these principles about written language long before they enter school. They learn them from road signs and advertising, from cereal boxes and other food containers, from games and toys, from television and from books. They learn them from the print that surrounds them, and from the ways in which they see adults using print. They do not learn them in a haphazard way, however. They are learned systematically over time because the environment in which print regularly occurs (its context of situation) is stable, and *together with* the print, that context serves to sign meaning potential. Observing young children interacting with natural language-using situations prompted Harste et al. (1984, p. 107) to conclude that:

> the decisions which children make in reading and writing from age 3 through age 6 are not only organised, but are laced with both personal and social organisation. This interplay between personal and social organisation in the evolution of literacy is universal.

Opportunities to use written language surround us as we go about our daily routines. Books, letters, magazines, television guides, advertising, junk mail, notes from one family member to another, computers, telephone books, greeting cards, shopping lists, video tapes, record albums, tickets—the list is endless. Children see 'literacy in action' as family members use various forms of written language over and over again. However, using written language is often a silent activity, not as easily shared with children as oral language, and they need to be included in written language activities as well. As Harste et al. (1984, pp. 42-43) say:

> The most salient home factor relating to literacy learning is one we have termed 'availability and opportunity to engage in written language events'. Homes where books were out and readily available, where pens, pencils, crayons, magic markers and other instruments were handy, where children seemed quite naturally to be included and involved, seemed to provide the key conditions for children to go exploring and for parents to involve themselves in using and encouraging reading and writing.... When papers and books were in the way, children used them, often coming up with quite creative uses (writing out a menu for supper, writing traffic tickets, writing notes, posting signs on doors, labelling their toys during play). When there were books in the family room, children were read to, an activity that seemed to be equally initiated by both parents and children.

The following vignettes of young written language learners would seem to support these assertions, as well as demonstrating some of the ways in which children can become socialized into literacy.

Learning about written language in the home and community

Hannah, 17 months, loves books. She carries her books with her all over the house and will sit and 'talk' her way, page by page, through book after favourite book. Her behaviour is not unexpected as her family read a great deal, and have shared books with her almost from birth. The interesting part of her behaviour is that she changes her 'talk' and tone of voice as she changes her books. Sometimes she drones, sometimes she sings, sometimes she names objects page by page. Hannah not only knows how to hold books and how they operate, but already seems to know that each one is different.

On Sunday Hannah is visiting her grandparents and the entire family is enjoying the weekend newspapers. As the family read the papers, they exchange the comics, comment on the news and discuss the cooking pages. Hannah watches for a few moments, then picks up part of the magazine section of the paper. She carefully turns the pages, keeping up a running vocalization to the paper as she does so. Then she brings her part of the paper to share with her mother: 'der tis,' she says pointing, 'der.' She performs this routine with anyone who is willing to listen to her, and then, picking up a new section of the paper, she repeats the process. As with her books, sometimes she focuses on a picture and sometimes she drones on and on before turning the page.

Everyone accepts Hannah's overtures with written language, just as they accept her approximations toward oral language. As Hannah involves herself as a member of her literate community, her inclusion as a literacy user is taken for granted.

Interacting with everyday reading resources.

Penny, 3, lives with her mother in the inner city. Her mother doesn't read to her and Penny owns only a couple of books. However, she does share in the written language for living that surrounds her. Her inner-city area has advertising, graffiti, and petrol station, shop and street signs, and her letterbox gets its share of junkmail. Penny is very aware of this print and often initiates conversations about it. Sometimes she and her mother eat out, and tonight they are going to McDonalds.

> PENNY: I'll show you the way, Mum.
> MUM: Okay, Penny. Which way do I go?
> PENNY: Drive past the Esso, then when you see K-Mart, go down there.
> (Penny's mother follows the directions.)
> MUM: Is that McDonalds? (pointing to a Pizza Hut).
> PENNY: No, silly! That's red and it's Pizza Hut. McDonalds has got yellow like this (making an M shape on the car window). Look! There's McDonalds.

Since families usually shop, or eat out, or buy petrol at consistent places, the experiences and the print of these encounters become predictable, and children become acutely aware of the print that is part of a particular context and activity. The environmental print their families use to go about their daily business is among the first written language that children recognize. They recognize it because of experience in using it for some purpose; and just as they assign meaning to language through experience as they learn oral language, so do they begin to recognise printed symbols as signing new meanings. Many of these symbols are also distinctive both in print form and colour. Penny at 3 is already using the print that is part of her experience to make sense of her world, displaying the functional principles identified in Yetta Goodman's research.

John, 5, is the elder of two children. His father owns a transport business and often takes John to work with him. His mother does the bookkeeping from home and frequently writes notes and telephone messages for her husband. Because of the long hours he works, John's father quite often gets home after the children are asleep. For some time he has been promising John a computer game, and John is worried that he may have forgotten about it. Prompted by the demonstrations of the uses of literacy that he sees in his home, John decides to remind his father of his promise by writing a note to his mother. He knows that such family messages are always read and acted upon. His writing shows a growing awareness of how written language is organized and his invented spellings show considerable insights into how words are formed.

```
MY DaD
SaID He
wooD Bye
Me a kam
Peutr Gam
on the        HaLL a pays
I wnDoor
wn He      IS
GoING to    Bye
It
```

Mark, Sam and Leata are 3 and 4 year olds who go to a day care centre which runs a pre-school program with parent help. The environment the children share is littered with written materials. The children use the environmental print of signs, foodstuffs and labels in their everyday activities; they share storybooks and nursery rhymes; they use their printed names to identify their belongings, and they 'write' notes to each other. The teacher and parents use print as an integral part of the routine of various activities wherever and however it is appropriate. Lately the children have been very interested in pet books. They have read and shared them and have looked after their budgie, Figaro, their two ducks, Defer and Bruce, and their long-suffering hen, Pinocchio. Spontaneously, a little group of children have decided to 'write' a shopping list of food for their pets, using the labels from empty food packets as models.

Writing up a shopping list from models.   *Reading the list to choose pet food.*

One of the parents, seeing the children's list, walked them to a nearby store, where they found and purchased the pet food, thus acting on their self-initiated written language experience.

Because these children are immersed in an environment that demonstrates literacy, they include it as a natural part of their learning experiences. They decide on the form it will take (in this case a list), how they will write it, and for what purpose. In Harste's terms, the materials of literacy are 'highly accessible', and so the children use them.

What conditions typical of oral language learning are revealed in these vignettes of written language learning?

- In all cases the children were *immersed* in environments which both invited and supported their responses to written language.
- The children's responses were based on *demonstrations* of written language in use by those around them.
- All children initiated the written language encounters, taking *responsibility* for their own learning by deciding which aspects of written language they wished to investigate.
- Although different, each situation offered opportunities for *employment* of written language as used by that particular family or group.

- In all cases the *feedback* was in direct response to the situation, providing the young written language learners with confirmation of the appropriateness of their efforts and the opportunity to try others.
- In each situation the children's *approximations* were recognized for what they were—growth in literacy learning—and they were accepted as such.

What are the implications for teachers in these vignettes?

Each situation was supported by a fairly predictable setting. Thus there were the familiar activities of:
- sharing newspapers
- retracing a well-known route
- writing notes
- caring for pets.

All situations were open-ended, and each participant was able to draw on prior knowledge and experience to initiate whatever literacy response was thought to be appropriate. More importantly, the literacy responses were at a level each could handle easily at his/her particular stage of literacy development.

Others sharing the situations simply assumed that the children's interest in literacy was a part of normal development. That development was highly individual, as the children responded to people and to features of the home and community environment.

In the natural settings of home and community literacy, *parents trust children as learners* and are *accepting of their responses to and explorations of literacy*. They regard children as informants and do not set out deliberately to teach them about literacy. Rather, they respond to children's initiatives. Parents are very competent 'kidwatchers', and kidwatching is a technique that could serve teachers equally well.

Why kidwatching?

It is clearly evident that children's expectations of the functions that literacy serves and the forms it takes will vary considerably, depending on the ways in which they have been socialized into literacy by their families and communities. If we are to learn from the insights of Goodman (1981), Harste, Woodward and Burke (1984), Brice Heath (1983) and others, then the teacher's major concern must be to recognize these different expectations and utilize them, as they will affect the ways in which children expand their use of language in a variety of settings and situations, and for a variety of purposes. A teacher informed about such expectations can better observe children to monitor their development as readers and writers, and to gain data on which to base planning for further literacy experiences.

Harste et al. (1984, p. 224) identify three requisites for such planning. Firstly, we need to understand theory—of how language is learnt and used successfully, and of how literacy develops. Secondly, we need to understand children as language informants, who show us how they are performing in relation to our knowledge of theory. Thirdly, we need to use our knowledge of theory and of children using language to decide the kind of curricular support we should offer to extend children's language-using capacities. To demonstrate an application of these requisites, let's discuss the vignette about John.

The theory

The theory supporting this chapter is that oral language acquisition is an interactive process, in which children discover how language is organized and used by participating actively in real, communicative situations; and that written language learning can be based on the same premises. John's case shows that written language learning is a self-generating, creative process, learnt not by explicit instruction but through experience—by listening to others, observing, and experimenting and practising in situations where written language serves genuine purposes.

The child as informant

From this theoretical perspective John is well on his way to becoming a successful written language user in the conventional sense. He shows his sensitivity to literacy use in his family by choosing to leave a written message for his mother to convey to his father, secure in the knowledge that messages in his household are always read. This decision, and his subsequent rather subtle wording, show that he knows why we use written messages and something about the form they can take. He is willing to 'risk take' as he hypothesizes about how written language is formed, and about possible spellings.

An informed kidwatcher would recognize what John already knows, and would plan experiences to build on that knowledge by introducing new concepts rather than focusing on his 'errors'. In this way John would continue to grow as a literacy user, confident in his developing ability, and with a sense of security that allows him to risk take. He would, we hope, continue to view literacy learning as an active, thinking process. (Note, however, that kidwatchers need to base their analyses on more than one instance—the example from John's vignette simply illustrates what can be inferred from observation informed by knowledge of theory.)

Curricular support

In a whole language classroom, which is the ideal learning environment envisaged here, the curriculum is, in Watson's (1985) words, 'the grist for the literacy mill'. Numerous curriculum areas would be integrated to support and nurture John's growing literacy awareness, as the following examples will show.

- The general classroom program would include many kinds of opportunities for the teacher and children to communicate through messages, notes, reminders and so on.
- In a science corner the teacher would leave written messages addressed to particular children, to remind them of things for which they are responsible in caring for a class pet. The teacher could include some procedural writing in the message:

  Dear John,
  Don't forget to feed the rabbit today.
  Take two big leaves of lettuce.
  Wash them in the sink and shake them dry.
  Open the door of the hutch and put them in quickly.
  Shut the door!
  Thank you, John.
  Mrs Bellugi

- In art and craft the children may need some particular scrap materials to create a fabric picture or collage. Children and teacher would compose and write a message to parents to be sent home with each child or made into a poster.
- As part of the preparation for an excursion the children would be involved in writing notes to parents. Thank-you notes would be written afterwards. Writing

reminder notes, lists of things to take on the excursion, and lists of what they might see or do would be literacy events occurring as a natural part of such an activity. Thus John would see many more real reasons for using written language and experience more of the different forms that it can take, as well as reinforcing and extending what he already knew about the purposes and forms of writing.

In any of these interactive experiences, the teacher would be 'kidwatching' to gather data for planning further learning experiences.

Kidwatching in the classroom

Three essential kidwatching focuses emerge from the findings of researchers such as Clay (1979), Goodman (1981; 1984), Harste, Burke and Woodward (1981), King and Rentel (1979), Calkins (1983) and Marek et al. (1984).

1—Observation

Observations can be designed to obtain specific information about language development, or they can take the form of general impressions the teacher gains over time. Anecdotal records which record the *data, setting, participants involved* and the *literacy incident* itself, form a valuable source of information, and allow the teacher to *sample* children across a range of *curriculum activities*. Anecdotal records can be used with individuals, a whole class, or a group. Here is one example of the form an individual anecdotal record might take.

Name: Mark *Date:* 3/4/86
Setting: Science area. Children looking at a poster they have made about the foods their pets eat, and discussing the labels on it.
Participants: Mark, Sam, Leata.
MARK: My dog likes Pal (*points to label*). That's Pal. (*He points to the print, then points to each letter.*) P - A - L. That says Pal.
SAM: (*running finger across the whole word* PAL) Yeah. That says PAL. PAL. PAL.
LEATA: My dog likes Whiskas.
MARK: Your dog's dumb.
LEATA: No. . . .

This minute or so of spontaneous interaction is a rich source of information for the teacher who knows these children well. At a superficial level, it is evident that Mark realizes that print carries the message, and that he is able to recognize some individual letters. And while the focus is on Mark, information about Sam and Leata can also be obtained from this observation.

The anecdotal record allows the teacher to evaluate a child's progress in a non-threatening environment, to note changes in growth and development in language, and to review many aspects of development such as attitudes, socialization and preferences, all of which are invaluable in planning for the child in a whole language program. A particular focus, such as willingness to risk take or assume responsibility, can be sometimes chosen, and anecdotes on every child can be collected to give a class profile. Anecdotal records with samples of the child's work at the time provide an excellent form of evaluation, as well as a focus for conferring with parents about their child's development.

2—Interaction

An interaction focus allows the teacher to gather information on the children's knowledge of language from the ways they use it in interactive situations, such as the following.

- *A shared book activity*, where knowledge can be gained, for instance, about individual children's ability to use the cueing systems of language to bring their prior experience of concepts and language to bear on making meaning. Knowledge about their book handling skills and familiarity with print conventions can also be gained.
- *A cooking activity*, where data can be gathered about children's understanding of the symbols and print on containers, or of the way a recipe is written.
- *Conferences* for reading, or editing, or publishing a book, all of which yield important data about children's language knowledge.

Interactions provide further opportunities to assess a child's language development, confirm observations, and gather information for analysis. The teacher needs to be an aware listener and reflect on what is *heard* in order to extend the child by probe questioning; and, above all, needs to be patient and let the child lead.

3—Analysis

Analysis of language use provides the teacher with an individual record of each child's development. Growth in the use of strategies—knowledge and use of print conventions, ability to use cueing systems, ability to predict, range of language used, invented spellings and so on—can all be documented through anecdotal records.

The focus of evaluation must always be on *content and process*, and on the opportunity for planning experiences and strategies to support continuing development. Evaluation must be *for* the child, just as parents' response to early efforts in language is *for* their children, in that it supports them in their learning. Kidwatching is a systematic follow-on from parenting, where parents, on a one-to-one basis, observe, respond to, and interact with their children.

Just as knowledge of research into early literacy learning can inform our classroom practice, so too can knowledge about how parents in our teaching community have socialized their children as literacy users provide valuable insights from which to plan further literacy experiences. The vignettes about Hannah, Penny, John, Mark, Sam and Leata clearly demonstrate the diversity of literacy experiences and expectations through which children can begin to become literacy users. This knowledge should tell us as teachers that because each child is an individual, the learning environments we plan should recognize individual learning through a range of contexts which support what children already know about language, while extending them to new realizations. Within these contexts, children should feel secure to risk take and hypothesize about language forms and functions as they negotiate meaning. Clearly the teacher's role is to be a facilitator and guide, rather than providing direct instruction.

Conclusion

Overwhelming evidence exists to support the view that children learn to use oral and written language through meaningful, interactive oral and written language experiences in their homes and communities. Mindful of the ways in which they learn, we need also to be aware of the diversity of oral and written language experiences that the children we teach may have encountered before they come to school, so that we can plan learning contexts and experiences that confirm for them the relevance of what they already know, while extending their knowledge to encompass new forms and functions of language use.

The contexts we provide for confirming and extending that knowledge should be rich in what Harste et al. (1984) termed the 'availability and opportunity to engage in written language events' by providing abundant writing and reading materials and ample opportunity to negotiate meaning with real purpose.

As oral and written language use varies according to its social context, we must also ensure that the contexts we provide enable children to experience a *comprehensive* range of language forms and purposes.

Within such a range of contexts reflecting meaningful and purposeful use of language, the informed kidwatcher can observe and respond to children's growing awareness about literacy, and use this as the basis for future planning. In this way, children can continue to learn about language in natural language environments which emulate the conditions under which they so successfully learn in the home and community.

3 Learning to Mean in Writing

Frances Christie
Deakin University

A great deal of children's learning involves the use of models: in learning behaviour appropriate to the meal table, the supermarket, the swimming pool, the school playground or the classroom, children are subtly socialized into various behavioural patterns, where they rely heavily upon the example of others in determining what they should do. Sometimes—quite frequently, in fact—aspects of the behavioural model are explained to children, by parent, teacher, sibling or peer, and sometimes they are simply adapted from observation of others. In both cases, however, it is clear that children learn to behave in appropriate ways by following the examples available to them in the patterns of other people's behaviour. The significance of modelling, of the consequences of the fact that we all do model our behaviour in various complex ways, is frequently not acknowledged properly in educational discussion. Yet it needs to be considered very seriously if we are to do justice to the learning needs of those whom we teach in schools. Never is this more the case than when we consider the practices of learning language, for language is itself a critically important resource in children's overall patterns of behaviour.

In general, language is probably not thought of as an aspect of behaviour at all. Certainly, if we were to conduct some sort of an opinion poll by asking people in the street what they thought language was, not many would identify it directly as a behavioural resource. Those professionally involved in the study of language—notably linguists—necessarily view the matter in other terms. Writers, actors and broadcasters have a professional interest in language as something with which they can move and excite people as well as inform them. They spend much of their lives perfecting the ways they use language, and to this extent they are conscious of language as an aspect of behaviour. Teachers too need a professional interest in the nature of language, for it is in language that so much that is typical of teaching/learning behaviour is *realized* or comes into being. In fact, language is a principal resource in the processes of school teaching and learning.

Learning to write is one aspect of learning language: like its companion, learning to read, it constitutes one of the most important learning tasks schools offer children.

While this observation is not one that many would challenge, it remains true that the significance of reading and writing as aspects of language behaviour is frequently not appreciated fully. Like any other areas of behaviour, they are learned from observation and practice in using the models of others.

Learning language as a social phenomenon

Much has been written since the 1960s about the processes by which young children learn their language, and it will not be necessary to review all of it here. Suffice it to note that this research, associated as it has been with a great deal of other linguistic, sociological and educational research, has thrown important light upon our understanding of the nature of human identity and experience.

Observation of the ways in which babies very soon after birth begin to interact with significant adults—mothers in particular—led Bullowa (1979) to argue that well before they are in control of a linguistic system, infants become 'conversational partners'. That is to say, through all the behavioural resources they rapidly develop, they are capable of responding to gesture, sound, facial expression and movement in a number of ways. As Halliday (1985b) puts it, they learn to 'sign'—a necessary step in the processes of learning to interact with others, and hence to make meaning, and an essential step on the way to the eventual learning of the mother tongue.

That children are able to learn to sign is entirely dependent upon the presence and very active cooperation of others. The parenting role is often understood as no more than a nurturing and comforting one, while an essentially passive role is assumed for the infant. But it is in their earliest relationships with parents and others that infants take their first steps in learning *what it is to behave at all*: what it is to respond to others, or to attempt to influence others. These are lessons having profound consequences for their ability to learn throughout their lives. Children learn primarily out of the need to interact with others in the constant endeavour to make sense of, and hence achieve some control over, their world. In this sense, all learning is social, and it is an extremely active process.

The ways in which children learn from the linguistic models of others in the processes of learning their mother tongue have been explored at considerable length by Painter (1985b).

In her study (1984; 1985a) she sought to replicate the earlier work of Halliday (1975) in investigating a young child learning his mother tongue. Studying her own son, Hal, from birth, she observed that he often employed linguistic models encountered initially in interaction with his parents. These he subsequently used himself in appropriate contexts, and where the associated meanings were relevant. One example will serve to illustrate the point. At the age of about 24 months, Hal and his mother engaged in the following discourse:

> MOTHER: Don't you want any tea? Do you want some cheese and biscuits?
> HAL: No.
> MOTHER: No? Not hungry. You're not hungry tonight, eh?

At 27 months, a conversation went thus:

> MOTHER: Want a bit of toast?
> HAL: No thanks I not hungry.
> (Painter 1985b)

We must assume that in the period between the two instances Hal had internalized the linguistic elements involved, and was thus able to use them himself. This example from Hal's early language learning is only one fragment from the total experience of such a child in mastering his mother tongue. The point to be noted, however, even in such a small example, is that having mastered the linguistic resources necessary to deal with the situation, he was enabled to act with greater independence than in the earlier episode. It is in this sense that the steady learning of the mother tongue enables children gradually to do more things. Learning language is a necessary part of learning to act with independence and consequently with power over the course one's life takes. When we teach children to use language, we assist in the process of developing people able to take power over their lives.

Learning to write as a social phenomenon

A familiar view of writing in our culture is that it is a means for people to 'develop individuality', and to 'be creative'. In this sense, it is seen as something very special—an art form, in fact—and teachers are often encouraged to see their role as that of fostering artistic or creative endeavour in their students. It is true, of course, that some forms of written language—the literary forms in particular—do constitute artistic achievements. One of the aims of Language Arts programs is for children to learn to write some literary forms of their own. However, there are in general two difficulties about a view of writing and its teaching which focuses primarily upon the activity as an artistic or creative endeavour. Firstly, it does a serious disservice to all the other forms of writing, mastery of which is a necessary part of schooling, and many of which are relevant to successful participation in the workforce later on. Secondly, the very special status often accorded to 'creative writing' tends to deny the role of any teaching activity in ensuring that children learn to write. An attitude often prevails, in fact, that the creative character of children's writing is such that it must not be 'interfered with' by teachers, and that children must be left free to develop their own written texts in their own ways.

The latter difficulty results from a confusion about the nature of 'creativity', while the former arises from a failure to take language seriously at all. In both cases, it is the absence of an appropriate sense of the social significance of language in the construction of experience which is at fault. To demonstrate the point it will be necessary to say a little more about the nature of language, particularly written language, as a social phenomenon.

We have already briefly alluded to the role of language in young children's negotiation of relationship and meaning in the early years of life. Whenever children like Hal learn language, they learn not only *how* to use certain linguistic items, but also *how to construct a meaning in the pattern they create with the linguistic items*. The two are in fact inseparable: meaning or 'content' comes into being in the language patterns selected. Thus it is that as children learn to use language, they actually learn ways of dealing with experience of many kinds. In the same sense, when children learn to write, they learn ways of dealing with experience in the written mode.

These ways of working are socially created: that is to say, they are not the creation of any one individual, but are rather created jointly by many people in the various social processes through which they interact with each other. So, for example, when people write, they select from one of a large range of possible written forms or genres: narratives, reports, sonnets, letters, argumentative essays, advertisements, notes, and so on. The number is potentially limitless, and there is good reason to believe that new genres are constantly being created because of the changing nature of society, and of the kinds of things people need to do with language. Each genre, having its own distinctive linguistic pattern or 'shape', is as it is because it represents another way of making meaning.

Children learn to deal with experience through writing.

The significance of this for educational experience can now be stated. School learning will always involve learning new ways of dealing with experience in some form or other, and they will be realised or created in differing linguistic patterns or genres. This will apply as much to learning to write literary pieces in Language Arts, as it will to writing about the concerns of the various other school subjects—notably Science and Social Science in the primary school. There is an important sense in which the school program—particularly the Language Arts part of it—will seek to develop creativity in children, enabling them to fashion literary pieces of their own. But in order to do this, children must be clear about what kinds of literary forms or genres are available for them to use. Once they have mastered the various features of the genres they need to use, they will become skilled at playing with them, and, sometimes, they will even create new ones.

What is a genre?

We will soon turn to look more fully at the processes of learning to write, and begin to examine some children's texts in the light of the observations above. But first we should pause to consider a more complete definition of the term 'genre'. Most people who know the term have met it in literary studies, where it has always been a familiar practice to speak of various literary genres: short stories, sonnets, odes, novels, plays, and so on. The term as used here is of course closely related to this original usage. However, it includes texts other than the numerous literary masterpieces normally encompassed in English literature courses. And it includes not only the potentially limitless range of written texts briefly alluded to above, most of which are not held to have any literary merit, but also a similar range of spoken texts. In fact, the linguistic theory invoked here (e.g. Kress 1982; Martin 1984; Hasan 1985; Christie 1985) suggests that every time people engage in some structured activity, interacting with others in a socially ordered manner, they construct a text which will be representative of one or other kind of spoken genre. One thinks, for example, of service encounters, and of the kinds of discourse patterns which apply when one goes shopping in markets, stores, post offices, and the like. But there are also spoken genres which apply when people visit the doctor, consult a lawyer, engage in debate on radio or television, conduct a public meeting, and last but by no means least, when teachers and students work together in classrooms. Successful participation in these various contexts of situation requires a capacity to use the appropriate linguistic patterns.

The claim made here, then, is that when children enter schools and begin learning to read and to write, they are actually engaged in learning the various written genres of their culture. If this is the case, it follows that teachers should have an appreciation of the kinds of genres relevant to school learning. Once they do appreciate the kinds of genres required, they will be able to teach them to children, helping them to identify and adapt appropriate generic models.

Children's first texts

The discussion of the previous chapter has already thrown useful light on ways teachers can begin establishing basic literacy. It stressed the importance of a supportive working atmosphere in the classroom, so that teachers and children share in the construction of texts, and this is in itself an acknowledgement of the social nature of the enterprise, and of the ways in which generic models for reading and writing should be jointly negotiated. While it is not intended here to traverse the territory covered in that chapter, we should say something about the first texts children produce, since they provide a necessary context for understanding subsequent development in learning to write.

Consider Text 1, written by Emily while she was in Grade 1.

Text 1   The Kittens

Today Wendy's mother came to show us the four kittens they wor cute one played wthi [with] Simon and one played with Jodie it was cute I pttd [patted] sum [some].

How might we characterize such a text—that is, what kind of genre does it appear to represent? What appears to be its function? Finally—an odd question, perhaps—where did it come from?

The text involves reconstruction of personal experience. It has an overall schema, and we can identify the principal elements in its *schematic structure*. They are:

Today Wendy's mother came to show us the four kittens	Observation
they wor cute	Comment
one played wthi Simon	Observation
and one played with Jodie	Observation
it was cute	Comment
I pttd sum	Observation

This is what Martin and Rothery (1984) call an Observation/Comment genre, an example of a kind of writing found very often in the infants' grades. Notice some of the linguistic features that contribute to the creation of such a text, entitling us to see some of the elements as Observation, others as Comment. (It should be noted that whenever a term is used with a capital letter in discussion of a text, as with Observation and Comment here, the capital marks the presence of a functional label, identifying a particular element in the schematic structure.)

The experiences dealt with are identified particularly in the verb choices. Those in the Observation elements are all what are called *material processes* (Halliday 1985a): they construct actions—*came to show*; *played* (used twice); and *pttd*. Those in the Comment elements are what are called *relational processes* because they construct processes of being—*were* (used twice). Both the elements identified as Comment have an item (the same one in fact) indicating Emily's attitude—*cute*. Finally, there are linguistic items in the text whose primary purpose is to help tie it together, justifying us in calling it a text, having coherence and unity. One such item introduces the text—*today*—and subsequently one conjunction—*and*—ties two clauses together. Otherwise, the linguistic items involved are mainly those which identify persons (*Wendy's mother*; *us*; *Simon*; *Jodie*; *I*) and those which identify things (*the kittens*, *they*; *one*; *it*; *sum*). Once Wendy's mother and the kittens have been introduced, they are not identified again by name, but referred to through the use of pronouns. The writer never identifies the people to whom she refers by using *us* (though *Wendy*, *Simon* and *Jodie* are clearly included) because, like a lot of young writers, she assumes her audience knows who they are. Overall, the pattern of identifying persons and things by naming them, and then referring back to them by using pronouns, contributes to the coherence of the text.

We have answered the first of the questions posed earlier by identifying the genre this text represents, but what can we say of its function? As we have noted, the text involves reconstruction of past experience. A very great deal of early writing by young children appears to involve such reconstruction of experience, and we might well ask why this is so. Where does it come from? Closer examination leads us to argue (Christie 1984; 1985) that such a pattern of reconstruction comes about because teachers provoke it, though they are not always conscious of doing so. Teachers tend to offer children an activity such as playing with and talking about kittens, and then to ask them to write about it: 'What did you do with the kittens? Who brought them to school? Did you like them?' and so on. What is to be noted here is that in posing such questions, teachers are actually pointing children in the direction of a particular generic choice. They are pointing towards the reconstruction of what happened, in a manner very like that in which adults will point children to talk by the kinds of questions they ask about what they have been doing, where they went, and whether they liked it. Children cannot write unaided, and they will look to the generic model available to them, even when teachers are not aware of it themselves, and they will attempt to use it as best they can.

The child in preparatory or infants grade who wrote Text 2 beneath a picture of himself—

Look at me. I'm Joel.

took the model available to him in the early reading program provided at his school. He was invited by his teacher 'to write a story about himself' in his first writing book, and in common with a number of his classmates, he selected a model from one of the few examples of written language he could read at that time. What he wrote is not in fact a 'story' at all, and if we are to accord it a status as a genre, then we should, like Martin (1985), call it a Labelling genre, thereby acknowledging that it has no real independence as a text, but is to be understood as accompanying the picture involved.

Recount genre

Reconstruction of experience may take forms other than the Observation/Comment genre identified above. Consider, for example, Text 3, written by Lucy in her first Grade.

> Text 3   Anakie Gorge
> *On Wednesday we went to Anakie Gorge and we went past Fairy Park and we walked half way and we found a koala and then we got to the picnic area and we saw another koala and then we clim[b]ed up the mountain and it was very steep and I slep [slipped] and we had lunch and we went for a walk near Stony Creek we collected some rocks that abrigins [aborigines] ues [use] to paint ther [their] skin with and befor[e] we went home we had a little play and some poeple [people] made som[e] dasiy chans [daisychains].*

This we will term a Recount genre (Martin and Rothery 1984). We call it a Recount because it involves reconstructing an actual series of events in which Lucy and her classmates participated. We may set out its schematic structure thus:

On Wednesday we went to Anakie Gorge	Orientation
and we went past Fairy Park	Event
and we walked half way	Event
and we found a koala	Event
and then we got to the picnic area	Event
and we saw another koala	Event
and then we climed up the mountain and it was very steep	Event
and I slep	Event
and we had lunch	Event
and we went for a walk near Stony Creek	Event
we collected some rocks that abrigins ues to paint ther skin with	Event
and befor we went home we had a little play	Event
and some poeple made som dasiy chans	Event

Consider the linguistic elements that make up this text, giving it its character as a Recount genre. The experiences dealt with in the Event elements are, with one exception only, identified in verbs making material processes: *went*; *walked*; *found*; *climed*; *collected*; *had a little play* (the one exception is at the point where a relational process is used in *it was very steep*). In other words, the experiences being recreated in this text are all actions, which by their nature are part of events. If we examine the way in which the text is tied together, so that Event follows upon Event, the most noticeable linguistic feature is the large number of items to do with time and the passage of time: *on Wednesday*; *and* (used several times with the sense of meaning *and then*); *then* (used twice); *before*. Typically, Recounts deal with the unfolding of a sequence of happenings over time.

Capacity to construct a Recount is very much dependent upon ability to recognise and select the linguistic items appropriate to the genre. As the analyses of Texts 1 and 3 have demonstrated, the two represent different genres, or two different ways to make meaning. Ability to construct such genres, exercising the appropriate linguistic choices, is learned. It is for teachers to understand the nature of these choices, the better to guide effective learning in their students.

Children learn to recount shared experience with teacher guidance.

Narrative genre

Now let us examine another text, representing yet another genre, written by Mandy.

> Text 4   Jamie and the Beanstalk
> *One day Jamie and he's [his] mother liv[e]d in a cottage by the(i)r self One day Jamie's mother sent Jamie to the marck [market] with the[i]r horse and on the way Jamie met a[n] old man the old man said can I have that cow Yes How much muny [money] Jamie said 20 dolis [dollars] ho no I'v[e] got sumthink [something] bet[t]er than 20 dolis how bowt [about] 9 magic beans Jamie fort [thought] Mum will be happy but when Jamie got home he's [his] mother said go to bed so Jamie went to bed and in the morning Jamie wok[e] up and saw a gr[e]at big beanstalk and start[ed] to clim[b] up in the kowd [cloud] and saw a casil [castle] and the dor [door] was open and Jamie went in and he saw a gos [goose] whot [what] lad [laid] go[l]den eggs and Jamie got the gos and ran but the giyint [giant] stepd [stepped] on him so Jamie did [died].*

This text we may classify as an example of the Narrative genre. As such, its overall schematic structure is very like that of many of the stories in spoken discourse analysed by Labov and Waletzky (1967). We may set out the schematic structure thus:

> *One day Jamie and he's mother livd in a cottage by ther self One day Jamie's mother sent Jamie to the marck with ther horse* .... Orientation
>
> *and on the way Jamie met a old man the old man said can I have that cow Yes How much muny Jamie said 20 dolis ho no I'v got sumthink beter than 20 dolis how bowt 9 magic beans Jamie fort Mum will be happy but when Jamie got home he's mother said go to bed* .... Complication
>
> *so Jamie went to bed* .... Resolution

and in the morning Jamie wok up and saw a grat big beanstalk and start to clim up in the kowd and saw a casil and the dor was open and Jamie went in and he saw a gos whot lad goden eggs and Jamie got the gos and ran but the giyint stepd on him .... Complication

so Jamie did .... Resolution

There are some linguistic elements of this text which compare with those of the Recount in Text 3. However, the texts do differ in quite significant ways, for they represent different ways to make meaning. Like Text 3, Text 4 has a series of events, and one of the most important linguistic factors responsible for this is the use of a large number of material processes: *livd; sent; met; go; start to clim; ran.* (The item *said* is classified as a verbal process, by the way, while *saw* is classified as behavioural, though both of them are very close to material processes.) Like the Recount, the text makes use of some items to do with the passage of time: *one day* (used twice); *and* (used in an *and then* sense on several occasions).

Narratives do typically involve some sequence of happenings through time. But there are several items tying the text together by means other than simple temporal connectedness, and their presence explains why a different kind of genre from a Recount is involved here. Narratives, unlike Recounts, will always involve some problem(s), some source(s) of difficulty, which in the nature of things also require(s) resolution. In this text, their presence is marked by the use of the conjunctions *but* and *so* (both used twice): *but when Jamie got home he's mother said go to bed so Jamie went to bed*, and again towards the end, *but the giyint stepd on him so Jamie did*. Items like *but* and *so* create causal connectedness between events, not temporal ones, and are critical to the pattern of building Complication and Resolution.

Narratives, like Recounts, deal with reconstruction of event and experience, though in the case of Narratives the experience dealt with is more often than not imaginary, while in Recounts it is typically drawn from real life. But there are of course many other ways to deal with experience apart from reconstruction, real or imagined.

Report genre

Simone, who was in Year 2 at the time, wrote Text 5, which is fundamentally different from the texts examined so far.

Text 5   Home Pride Baker

A Home Pride Baker wears a hat a green dress, and a badge that says Home Pride bread it is sopposed [supposed] to look nice and if they dont wear thier [their] clothes they can't do thier work. If you don't wear a hat some of your hair might fall in the bread.

Text 5 represents a Report genre, a text in which the intention is to provide an explanation (or perhaps we should say an exposition) about the practice of having bakers—specifically Home Pride ones—wear uniforms while they work. The text was written as part of a Social Science unit of work on clothing, uniforms in particular. We may set out its schematic structure thus:

A Home Pride Baker wears a hat a green dress, and a badge that says Home Pride bread .... Generalization

it is sopposed to look nice .... Explanation

and if they dont wear thier clothes they can't do thier work   Explanation

If you don't wear a hat some of your hair might fall in the bread   Explanation

What linguistic features give this text its particular character as an expository piece—that is, a text dealing with factual information of some kind? Most of the processes used are again material: variants upon *wears*. The Recount and the Narrative we examined also used a majority of material processes, so they have this much in common with Text 5, though it remains a very different text from the earlier two. In particular, it is the use of the present tense rather than the past tense in Text 5 which accounts for the difference in meaning. In the English language, the present tense is used typically in texts dealing with the world of publicly verifiable fact or information, so that it is a frequent feature of expository texts. The past tense belongs more typically to texts dealing with the reconstruction of event or experience—hence its role in Texts 3 and 4.

In terms of overall schematic structure, there is much to commend in Text 5. As is conventional in such expository writing, Simone begins with an element (the Generalization) whose function is to create a general statement or proposition. The function of the subsequent elements (identified as Explanations) is to support or expand upon the opening Generalization.

The need for models of expository text

At the time of writing Text 5 Simone had had relatively little experience in writing such expository texts. Her teachers in Years 1 and 2 tended instead to encourage her to write Recounts and Narratives. Like many other teachers of young children, they assumed that Recounts and Narratives were more appropriate to her age. Indeed, many teachers assume that factual or expository writing is too difficult for young children, and that it should not be introduced till they have been at school some years. There is no real evidence to support such an assumption. Expository writing in itself offers no more substantial challenge to the young writer than does Narrative, provided the generic models are made available.

Perhaps it was Simone's relative inexperience in writing such texts that caused her to use the jumble of linguistic items she selected to refer back to her subject or theme: namely 'a Home Pride Baker'. She uses *it*—an item with which she intends to refer to the whole uniform she has described in the first sentence; subsequently she refers to *they*, thus switching from singular to plural; and finally she writes of *you* when talking of the purpose in having bakers wear a hat. This inconsistency in her choice of pronouns would not even be remarked upon, probably, if she were talking. But the demands of written language are considerably different from those of speaking. The items involved are very important in this text. Their function, like that of similar items earlier identified in Text 1, is to tie the text together, referring back in the Explanation elements to *a Home Pride Baker* in the opening Generalization element.

Were Simone given more opportunity to read models of appropriate factual written language, as well as to practise writing such genres herself, she would certainly improve in her control of the linguistic patterns required. However, the kinds of books typically written for young readers in their first few years of school do not on the whole offer models, good or bad, of factual written language. Overwhelmingly, they appear to offer narrative genres, and to a lesser extent, Recount ones. It would seem that most book publishers assume that young children cannot cope with the demands of factual writing: that the activity of exploring factual experience, whether it be aspects of one's neighbourhood and community, or details of clothing and why it is worn, or, perhaps, how things are made, is in some way too hard.

This is a curious assumption if one takes into account the many areas of factual experience with which children patently do cope satisfactorily in their daily living and talk. They normally negotiate their own neighbourhood reasonably well, making friends, moving to and from school, using local shops; they learn to identify many aspects of the ways people around them behave, how they conduct businesses and adopt relevant clothing where needed; they learn and know a great deal about the working of the supermarket, the post office and the public transport system, though adults are usually present when they use them. In other words, there is a great wealth of information available to children—or alternatively, capable of being made available to children through the agency of schooling—to do with factual experience of, and exploration in, the world about them.

It is true, of course, that many schools and teachers do try to tap such information and experience in their early language programs with children. However, the present writer at least would assert firstly that the print material available for young children to read about such matters is poor and very scanty, and secondly, that the incentive or opportunity given to children to write factual material is also very limited. Writing about a visit to the community, for example, whatever were the objects in undertaking it, generally becomes no more than a Recount. Indeed, there are primary teachers who, when challenged, will acknowledge that Recount is the principal genre they ask of their children throughout all the years of schooling. If this is so, it is a sad commentary on the very limited range of genres children are enabled to recognize and use, and hence, upon the limited range of factual meaning they are encouraged to make in writing.

Curriculum differentiation and its demands

Text 5 was written by a child in Year 2, as we have already noted, and in a few months she would enter Year 3. Typically, Year 3 is seen as the year of transition from the infants school to the primary school, and from that point of view it is often perceived as an important one. Whatever may be the merits of the claim that school becomes very different at Year 3, it is clear that the general tendency of schooling beyond the infants years and into the upper primary and secondary school is that the curriculum areas become more clearly differentiated. Science, Social Science, Language Arts, Mathematics, and so on, become recognizably different content areas, whereas in the early years it is often impossible to make distinctions between curriculum areas.

One consequence of the steady differentiation into the various curriculum areas, which begins about Year 3, should be that teachers give careful thought to the differing kinds of reading and writing experiences they plan for their students. Indeed, if the school program is working properly, children should learn to write and read a wide range of written genres, factual ones in particular, to deal adequately with the various school subjects. We will now examine some texts from Years 3 and 4, with a view to considering what might be some of the written genres of importance in the 'middle years' of primary schooling. Text 6 was written by Christine in Year 3.

Text 6   Ireland

Fact's about Ireland

Languages: English and Gaelic.

Head of Government. Prime Minister.

The National Anthem. The Soldier's Song.

Ireland's Flag dates from the 1800's. Green represents the country's Roman Catholics Orange the Protestants of Ulster and white, unity.

Ireland is a republic with a President, a Prime Minister and a parlament.

> <u>The people of Ireland</u> are warm and friendly and never rush.
> <u>The climate of Ireland</u> is never very hot and never very cold.
> <u>The Emerald Isle</u> is a small but long river in Ireland.

This is immediately recognizable as an expository text, dealing with factual information. The child's use of underlinings indicates steps in the overall plan, which were provided by the teacher. Their presence of course marks the text as very different from a Narrative, or any of the other texts we have already examined. In terms of overall schematic structure, the text constitutes a series of Descriptions. The processes used are relational, and have to do with assertions about what *is* factually so. The text is written in the present tense, a characteristic of factual writing, as we have noted.

The model for the genre used here almost certainly came from the kinds of entries often found in encyclopedias, particularly those written for school children. It is this model which accounts for the somewhat displeasing lack of continuity from element to element of the text. Linguistically, there are few items tying it together in a coherent way. The item 'Ireland' itself is repeated frequently, and together with the series of underlined headings, accounts for what little sense of overall unity the text has.

Why might a teacher involve children in writing such a text? Part of the explanation may lie in the availability of the model found in many encyclopedias. But that only begs a wider question: why create such genres at all? The overall lack of continuity implies an uncertain purpose in writing. In defence of the teacher, we may note that she did seek to provide a model, and that the use of subheadings provides a potentially useful structure. None the less, the text is not a happy one, and like the encyclopedia entries of which it is reminiscent, we would suggest that it is not a desirable model to offer children to write. They need to be encouraged to write texts in which the linguistic requirement for coherence is much greater, so that the interest of the facts, whatever they are, is given a better directed focus. It is imperative that children be offered good models for the construction of expository genres, because they are such an important part of many areas of school learning.

Developing control over expository text

Now let us consider Text 7, by Rebecca, in Year 4, which constitutes a Report.

> Text 7   Cassowary
>
> A cassowary is a bird, a very fierce bird. It is fierce because it's got feet and at end of the feet it has got claws like daggers. It is found in New Guinea and Australia. The cassowary is the only bird known to kill someone.

This is in every way a more satisfying text than Text 6, because it has a greater sense of unity and purpose. Its schematic structure may be set out thus:

> A cassowary is a bird, a very fierce bird . . . .   Generalization
>
> It is fierce because it's got feet and at end of the feet it has got claws like daggers . . . .   Description
>
> It is found in New Guinea and Australia . . . .   Description
>
> The cassowary is the only bird known to kill someone . . .   Description

One significant linguistic element responsible for the sense of unity in this text is the skill with which Rebecca uses her *referential items* to refer back to the item which is theme for the whole text, namely *a cassowary*. The items are all instances of *it*:

it is fierce; it's got feet; it has got claws; it is found. Then Rebecca finishes by thematizing *the cassowary* in the last sentence. Enough has been said of the linguistic features in earlier texts to enable the reader here to identify the linguistic features which make this an expository text—in particular, its large number of relational processes and its use of the present tense.

Next we will examine a text by Naomi, a Year 5 student. It is another example of a Report.

Text 8 Macaws

Macaws are brightly colored parrots. They live in the jungles of South America. They have a large hooked bill half of the size of their head. Macaws also have very long tails almost as long as their body. They have bare feathers except for a few tiny feathers these bare spots blush when a macaw gets exited. Macaws choose a partner and stay together for life. They feed on fruit, seeds and nuts. Macaws nest in the hollows of trees, here 2 or 3 eggs are laid. The female sits on these eggs for more than a month. When the chicks have hatched they have a very big beak for their size and only a few feathers. Chicks stay in the nest for more than 3 months before they are big enough to leave. Some macaws have been known to live up to 50 years old.

In terms of schematic structure, this text begins with an opening Generalization, and subsequent elements constitute Descriptions. The text has a pleasing sense of unity. One factor responsible for this, as in Text 6, is the writer's control of the various referential items. *Macaws* is theme, of course, both for the text overall, and for the opening sentence. Subsequent referential items—notably *they*—are used to refer back to it. Later, *the female* and *the chick* are both thematized, and they are also well referred to in following pieces of the text. A number of the processes here are material, forming parts of the ways the habits of the birds are built up in the text: e.g. *feed*; *nest*; *sits*. Elsewhere, some processes are relational, again a feature of a text which sets out to assert what is factually the case: e.g. *are* and *have* in *they have a large hooked bill*.

Like Text 7, this represents an example of one of the many kinds of expository writing that schooling should introduce to children. The child who wrote it had been properly taught, and encouraged to use appropriate models for the construction of such genres.

To return to the example of Text 6 above, which we identified as a less pleasing piece of writing—it might be suggested that its shortcomings, compared with those of Texts 7 or 8, result from the writer being younger rather than anything else. There is a time-honoured assumption (which does of course have some truth) that children's development as writers is such that with greater maturity they can do many things which they could not do earlier. Hence, this would suggest, younger children will produce more limited kinds of genres than older students because they lack maturity. But such an assumption can trap us into making some hasty judgements. Most notably, it often causes teachers to neglect to teach certain generic models to their students on the grounds that they are 'too difficult': where this happens, obviously, the children do not learn the models. The writer of Text 6 had been offered a bad model, as we suggested earlier, while the writers of Texts 7 and 8 had both been taught better and more satisfying models. That this is not a matter of age, but of experience and opportunity—*of what has been taught*, in fact—may be confirmed when we consider our final text, Text 9, written by Jodie at the same age as Naomi, who wrote Text 8, and also in Year 5.

> Text 9   China
> *In China it is mainly sunny. Their house's are made out of tin and brick The women plant rice in a certain time of the month they put in mud so it grow better Rice is very popular in China. At China the men fish a lot.*

We will not analyse this text in any detail, only commenting that it has a displeasing lack of continuity. Linguistically, it does not have a sense of overall coherence and unity, so that it appears poorly organized and unfocused. Yet we would argue that if the child was capable of eliciting even this amount of information from whatever sources were consulted to construct the text, she was also able, with appropriate support from a teacher, to put it together into a linguistically more satisfactory text.

Conclusion

It is time to bring this discussion to a close. We began it with an observation that a great deal of children's learning involves mastery of a range of behavioural models. We suggested further that nowhere is this more apparent than in the case of learning language. Learning to be literate is one very important aspect of learning language. When we examine closely the kinds of tasks children have to be able to undertake in language as they learn both to write and to read, we discover that these tasks require mastery of a range of differing linguistic patterns. Each linguistic pattern leads to the production of a text, and in turn each text will be an example of one or other kind of genre: one or other way of making meaning in language. Such genres are capable of analysis and description. If teachers are to succeed in teaching their students the various genres of schooling, it is imperative that they themselves are able to recognise and analyse them. They will then be able to plan writing programs properly, intervening in the processes by which children learn to write, and guiding them towards appropriate generic models. The processes of teacher intervention and guidance should start from the earliest months of schooling, and go on through all the years of subsequent school experience. Increasing proficiency and success in school learning will be very intimately related to increasing capacity to master the range of relevant written genres in which the knowledge of school is realized or brought into being.

4 Connecting Writing and Reading

Michèle Anstey
Darling Downs Institute of Advanced Education

This chapter explores aspects of the interrelatedness of reading and writing. Through the ideas presented, teachers should be able to plan and implement a literacy program which teaches children *how* to use reading and writing *to learn* in all curriculum areas. Since learning through writing and reading includes learning how to explore ideas, to marshal information and to construct meaning and knowledge in different ways, such a program will employ varied text types derived from content across curriculum areas.

Reading and writing: two complementary processes

Several authors (e.g. Tierney and Pearson 1983; Squire 1983) have written about similarities between the reading and writing processes. Some of these were discussed in Chapter 1. More recently, Hornsby, Sukarna and Parry (1986, p. 115) have synthesized what readers and writers do as they interact with text in this way:

The reader:	The writer:
reconstructs	*constructs*
another's meaning	own meaning
(comprehends)	(composes)

They suggest that while reading, we do not simply decode words or encode some meaning inherent in a text. Rather, we intend to reconstruct the writer's meaning. In these terms, reading comprehension includes the act of 'looking over the writer's shoulder', to reflect upon what the *writer* intended to mean.

Similarly, while writing, we do not simply compose with words. We construct textual meaning from experience and knowledge of language, content and text features, so that potential readers will understand our *intended* message. To achieve this effect, we write as a *reader* reconstructing our personal meaning with the intention to share understanding.

Anstey and Bull (1986, p. 3) extend the idea of this writer-reader interaction with text during composing and comprehending by suggesting that:

The reader	The writer
reconstructs	constructs
another's meaning	own meaning
(comprehends)	(composes)
and in so doing	having used others' ideas
constructs	and own experiences
his/her own meaning	and
	reconstructs
	meaning

Thus they highlight how readers 'write', and writers 'read' in complementary ways to create personal and shared meanings. It follows then that writing and reading texts in classrooms should be complementary activities, the major objective of which is to facilitate learning through and about both.

Two concepts, those of intention and interaction, are fundamental to understanding composing and comprehending as complementary processes in constructing and reconstructing meaning through text. Effective writers and readers have *intentions* to share textual meanings. They fulfil their intentions by *interacting* with a common text.

To do so successfully, we must probe what it is possible to do as writers and readers creating meaning intentionally. Opposite, by means of a diagram, some possible processes involved in writing and responding to the narrative excerpt given below are explored hypothetically. (While they may not reflect E. B. White's actual intentions as a writer, this is not the purpose of the example.)

> As time went on, and the months and years came and went, he was never without friends. Fern did not come regularly to the barn any more. She was growing up, and was careful to avoid childish things, like sitting on a milk stool near a pigpen. But Charlotte's children and grandchildren and great-grandchildren, year after year, lived in the doorway. Each spring there were new little spiders hatching out to take the place of the old. Most of them sailed away, on their balloons. But always two or three stayed and set up housekeeping in the doorway.
>
> Mr Zuckerman took fine care of Wilbur all the rest of his days, and the pig was often visited by friends and admirers, for nobody ever forgot the year of his triumph and the miracle of the web. Life in the barn was very good—night and day, winter and summer, spring and autumn, dull days and bright days. It was the best place to be, thought Wilbur, this warm delicious cellar, with the garrulous geese, the changing seasons, the heat of the sun, the passage of swallows, the nearness of rats, the sameness of sheep, the love of spiders, the smell of manure, and the glory of everything.
>
> Wilbur never forgot Charlotte. Although he loved her children and grandchildren dearly, none of the new spiders ever quite took her place in his heart. She was in a class by herself. It is not often that someone comes along who is a true friend and a good writer. Charlotte was both.
>
> (E. B. White, *Charlotte's Web*)

Connecting Writing and Reading

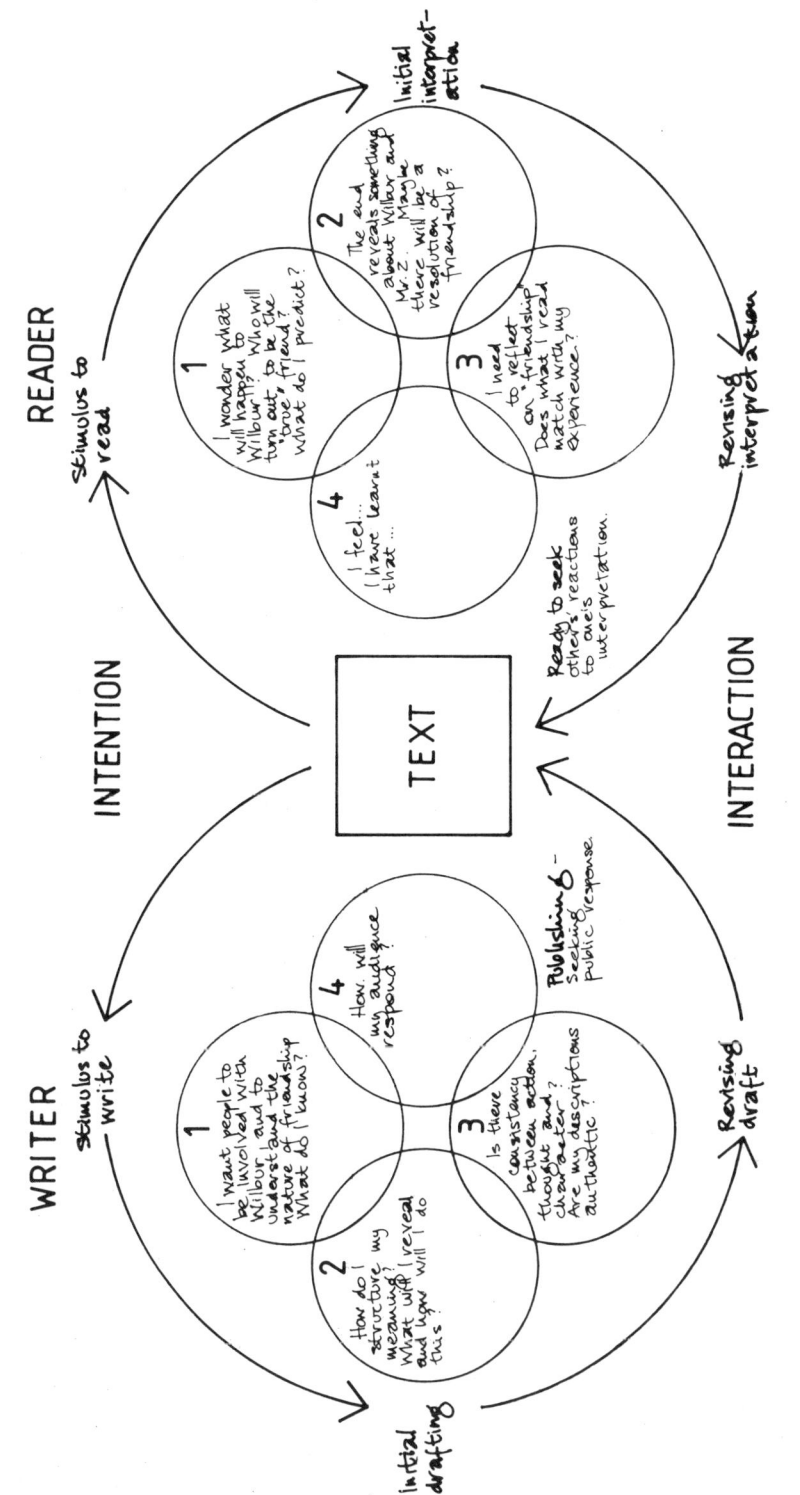

In the diagram, circling around the writer's and reader's 'thoughts' are the reading and writing processes in which they engaged. When one compares the writer's processes with those of the reader, the similarities between the two are further exemplified.

To the left and right are depicted some possible thoughts occurring to both writer and reader as they intend to interact with the text. To fulfil their intentions both invoke metacognitive processes: they monitor their reactions to and interactions with the text. It is this monitoring of thinking which aids clarification through composing and comprehension of text. By doing so, both writer and reader achieve two goals:

(1) each constructs and reconstructs personal meaning
(2) each develops understandings of a concept: in this instance, that of friendship.

General teaching implications can be derived from these points about monitoring composing and comprehending processes. They include the value of reading and writing experiences to:

(1) understand and promote thinking and learning
(2) teach/learn concepts
(3) extend the quality and range of textual interaction in different subject areas.

Exploring writing (and reading) as learning

Writing has always been used in subject areas other than Language Arts, but the intention of writing in these disciplines has not always focused on the process of learning. For example, writing has been used as an instrument for measuring what has been learned, in the form of short and long answers to questions about content read in text. It has included transcribing, note-taking and summarizing the ideas of others. While these activities serve useful purposes, they tend to focus on content acquisition rather than on how ideas might be shaped and organized through cognition and language. Learning therefore has not been maximized. To maximize learning through writing, we need to go beyond note-taking, which is only a first stage in the learning process (and of the writing process—that is, note-taking is a pre-writing activity, assembling information and ideas about which to write).

Writing to learn should involve those activities we traditionally reserve for reading comprehension: synthesizing learning by making inferences, drawing conclusions, and applying knowledge to new situations. As with reading, writing-to-learn activities can be used to acquire information and generate knowledge. They can also be used to process knowledge—as part of the process of learning to make connections; to hypothesize, infer and draw conclusions; to consolidate and apply knowledge gained to new situations, and to evaluate one's understanding at the end of the learning cycle. Examples of such activities at each stage of the learning process thus defined include:

Acquiring/Generating Knowledge
- note-taking
- graphing
- keeping diaries/journals
- writing definitions
- transcribing

Writing and graphing to process knowledge.

Processing/Making Connections	• collating notes • identifying cause/effect relationships • grouping similar information together (clustering) • constructing flow charts, retrieval charts
Drawing Conclusions/ Hypothesizing	• writing a report on an experiment conducted • answering inferential questions • writing a summary of information on a graph • writing a description of a flow chart or retrieval chart • posing questions/problems • exploring possible solutions
Consolidating and Applying Knowledge to New Situations/ Evaluating one's Learning	• writing in the form of text being learned about (e.g. haiku) • writing a fictionalized account of an event, using knowledge acquired • writing in the role of a person from another era or in another situation • writing a solution to a proposed problem • designing and writing a proposal for an experiment related to information acquired • using information acquired to write a different solution to a problem.

Such a range of writing-to-learn activities involves children in reading about and organizing ideas in writing in different ways. Since much learning takes place through reading and writing interaction with a range of text types, it is clearly important for children to learn about and experience a variety of them.

Different types of text for reading, writing and learning

To plan and teach effective literacy programs we need to employ a range of different types of text which serve different purposes. To realize meaning, and thus *learning* through texts, requires intentionally thoughtful interaction with them as readers *and* writers. Further, if children are to engage with reading and writing to learn in subjects beyond Language Arts, they need to understand those types of text which shape and convey particular subject information. A balanced program will incorporate varieties of written texts appropriate to the learning objectives and the curriculum area being focused on at a given time.

It is necessary therefore to identify a range of texts with which children may engage in the course of their content learning. This will enable appropriate literacy experiences to be developed to maximize children's learning across the curriculum areas.

To help identify and choose appropriate texts for teaching and learning through reading and writing, I have drawn on a variety of sources to identify five text types I consider necessary for inclusion in balanced curriculum units. Because I am concerned to include 'everyday' utilitarian texts in curriculum planning, I have included them in my 'procedural' category, and have differentiated others to serve my planning framework purpose. Categories are not discrete, and depending on intention and audience, texts may fit into more than one.

Identifying Types of Text

Types of Text	Procedural	Expository	Personal	Narrative	Artistic
Intention	To direct activity	To inform	To explore oneself	To entertain	To share language as an artform
Audience	Others	Others	Self	Others	Others

Within each general category, however, it is possible to distinguish specific text examples. Thus, what I have interpreted as 'procedural' text includes those examples which enable people to carry out tasks. They set out guidelines for providing data and for following the procedures involved in a particular activity. For instance, forms enable people to provide information to others so that payments may be made and collected, complaints registered, applications processed; directories enable people to locate telephone numbers and streets; sets of instructions enable people to assemble parts and to make things; and so on. The table below lists some examples of specific texts within each general category.

Procedural	Expository	Personal	Narrative	Artistic
• directories • forms • lists • instructions • problems • some diaries	• encyclopedias • atlases • reference books • non-fiction • reports	• some verse • informal notes for oneself • stream of consciousness writing • learning logs • personal diaries	• mystery • science fiction • fantasy • adventure • realistic fiction • fairy tales • myths and legends	• plays • haiku • odes • ballads • limericks • sonnets

It will be noticed that diaries appear as both personal and procedural texts. The reason for this dual placement is as follows: a personal diary would have as its intention 'exploring oneself—a daily record and exploration of one's thoughts, feelings, reactions and activities. A procedural diary, on the other hand, might be used by a business person or, to use an historical example, an explorer. Its intention would be to direct activity—to log daily actions or plan future ones. Because the diary might be needed for future reference, it would have to be organized for ease and efficiency of reference. The audience for such a diary, in the first instance, would be self, but because of its writer's several intentions, it may eventually be anyone. The explorer's diary, for example, could be used during the journey to log all that occurred, detailing the journey and the territory discovered; after the journey it could be used to aid the explorer's report writing for government and sponsors; in the future, it might be viewed as an expository historical document which other readers use to inform themselves about the explorer, his journey and what he discovered. Thus, writer-reader intentions and interactions with a text determine in this instance how we might categorize it. As indicated earlier, categories are not necessarily discrete.

It is believed that to learn through writing and reading, children need to become familiar with a range of texts used in different curriculum areas. Below are listed examples of text appropriate to Social Studies, Science and Maths. The examples are representative only; the list is not exhaustive.

Type of Text	Social Studies	Science	Maths
Procedural	• diaries • graphs • forms	• diaries • graphs • problems	• problems • graphs
Expository	• encyclopedias • reference books • atlases • non-fiction books	• reports • summaries	• reports • summaries
Personal	• personal diaries • learning logs	• observation notes • learning logs	• notes to oneself • learning logs
Narrative	• adventure • fantasy • historical fiction • myths and legends	• fantasy • science fiction	• counting books • fairy tales
Artistic	• ballad • haiku • sonnet • plays	• rhymes	• nursery rhymes

An elaboration of how diaries, adventure and fantasy fiction, fairy stories, rhymes and ballads might be used to foster learning is shown in the next table. In each instance, children would need to explore, by recursive reading and writing of their own and others' texts, the concepts to be learned.

	Social Studies	Science
Procedural	Processing and applying information about early explorers through writing DIARY accounts of their travels	Recording in DIARY changes/growth in an experiment over a period of time
	Reading a DIARY account of life in the penal colony to learn about the period	Interpreting DIARY records of an experiment

	Social Studies	Maths
Narrative	Writing about the adventures and life of a child in another culture in order to process and apply knowledge (ADVENTURE FICTION)	Writing a FAIRY STORY that uses the number seven to consolidate cardinal value
	Reading *Playing Beattie Bow* (Ruth Park) to understand life in early Sydney (FANTASY FICTION)	Reading FAIRY STORIES that concentrate on three to consolidate cardinal value ('Billy Goats Gruff', 'Three Bears', etc.)
Artistic	Processing and applying knowledge to write a BALLAD about the Eureka Stockade	Writing a cumulative rhyme to reinforce multiplication skills (RHYMES)
	Reading *The Oath of Bad Brown Bill* (Steven Axelson) to promote understanding of bushrangers in Australian history (BALLAD)	Reading and dramatizing NURSERY RHYMES dealing with numbers to reinforce cardinal values

Planning reading and writing to learn activities in a range of subject areas

Two illustrative units, designed to demonstrate the integration of learning through writing and reading, are outlined below. The content for each derives from curricula appropriate for the middle primary years. Although the presentation format varies slightly from subject to subject, the planning sequence is the same.

1. Flow charts show the 'brainstorming' which led to the planned focus for each unit. They identify:
   (a) the unit topic and purpose
   (b) the knowledge to be acquired in terms of
      (i) specific content and/or facts necessary
      (ii) the learning processes being developed, including the text types explored through associated reading and writing
   (c) the application/evaluation of knowledge acquired—activities which involve children in synthesizing and using knowledge in new situations.
2. Specific activities from the beginning, middle and end of the respective units show the purpose of each activity, its specific objectives, strategies, resources and evaluation procedures.

Example 1 Social Studies

Topic: exploration immediately after the first settlement in Australia.
Purpose of Unit: children will understand the problems of the first settlement which led to exploration. They will understand the reasons for and purposes of exploration. They will make connections between past and present-day exploration.
Major Generalization: changing needs of the Australian population led to exploration of new areas.
Specific Topic: the crossing of the Blue Mountains.

FLOW CHART OF UNIT

```
                    Knowledge
                   ↙         ↘
      Specific Content    Processes being
                          Developed
```

Specific Content	Processes being Developed	Application/Evaluation of Knowledge Acquired
• Population of first settlement • Needs of first settlement • How needs were met • Formation of first settlement • Land use • Reasons for exploration • Names • Dates • Discoveries • Effects of discoveries on first settlement	• Finding information • Identifying main ideas • Making inferences • Critical thinking • Analysing • Hypothesizing • Detecting bias • Distinguishing fact/fiction *Written Texts being Used/Developed* • Procedural —diaries —note-taking —graphing —mapping • Expository —reports —non-fiction —reference books —encyclopedias • Narrative —historical fiction —fantasy fiction • Artistic —ballads —songs —plays	• Write a diary account of the crossing of the Blue Mountains. • Write a report from the governor of the new settlement to Britain explaining the need for exploration. • What sort of exploration goes on now? • What are the purposes of current exploration? Are any of these purposes similar to those studied in the first settlement? • How did life change in the settlement as a result of exploration? • Write an *imaginative letter* from someone in the settlement to Britain describing the changes which took place between the time of the first settlement and the first journeys of exploration.

Activity 1: Beginning of Unit
Purpose: a focusing activity to provide the children with a context for the unit of work they are commencing. It is designed to activate knowledge the children already have about the first settlement in Sydney, and to enable them to understand the differences between living in the first settlement and present-day life.

OBJECTIVES	STRATEGIES	EVALUATION
General • Develop an understanding of life in the first settlement. *Specific* • Identify features of family life in early settlement. • Compare these features with present-day life. • Use fiction as a learning resource. • Construct a retrieval chart. • Use maps as a source of information.	• Read children parts of *Playing Beattie Bow* (Ruth Park). • Use discussion to identify differences between the life of the Bow family and Abigail's present-day life. • Construct a retrieval chart representing these differences. • Point out that in part this book is set in the 1870s, which was almost 100 years after first settlement. Consider what life was like prior to the 1870s. • Examine maps of area—old and new. Discuss differences.	• Did children identify features of life in the 1870s family and present-day family? • Were children able to suggest ways of constructing a chart to show differences? • Did children identify differences between old and present-day maps? **RESOURCES** • Ruth Park, *Playing Beattie Bow* (Puffin 1982). • Maps. • Materials for chart.

Activity 2: Middle of Unit
Purpose: to synthesize specific information acquired about the search for a suitable crossing of the Blue Mountains; to emphasize the difficulties experienced in early exploration as opposed to some present-day exploration (i.e. primitive technology for food preservation, transport, navigation, etc.).

OBJECTIVES	STRATEGIES	EVALUATION
General • Identify the main features of the expedition crossing the Blue Mountains and the difficulties encountered. *Specific* • Write in a procedural-type diary. • Present information in the correct sequence. • Present information appropriate in terms of the period and knowledge of the journey. • Identify and emphasize appropriate problems associated with the expedition.	• Review through time-line the main features of the Blue Mountains expedition. • Review features of diary writing with reference to diaries used in acquiring information about the expedition and children's personal diaries—discussion and demonstration. • Review the differences between the Blue Mountains expedition and a similar expedition now—discussion and blackboard summary. • Ask children to commence writing a diary account of the Blue Mountains expedition as though they were one of the party. Remind them to develop authenticity by 'discussing' problems as well as events.	*Pre-writing activities* • Contributions to discussion of sequence; features of expedition; problems encountered. *Diary writing* • Was text type used effectively and conventionally? • Did the child identify the correct sequence of the expedition and its main features? • Was the period authentically portrayed? • Did the child identify appropriate problems associated with the expedition in writing? **RESOURCES** • Examples of diaries. • Flow chart materials. • Blackboard.

Activity 3: End of Unit
Purpose: an evaluation activity, requiring children to demonstrate that they have developed an understanding of why exploration is necessary. It will also evaluate specific knowledge they have learned about a particular exploration and why it was necessary. The activity requires children to synthesize specific knowledge, draw conclusions and put themselves in the place of someone in another period—that is, to empathise.

OBJECTIVES	STRATEGIES	EVALUATION
General • Demonstrate knowledge of reasons for exploration. *Specific* • Identify specific reasons for exploration after the first settlement was established. • Write a report. • Demonstrate empathy with a person in another period. • Write appropriately for a given audience and purpose.	• Review report writing —features/purposes —setting out. • Look at governors' reports written during the first settlement. • Explain to children their task is to write a report in the role of governor: its audience is the British government. • The purpose of the report is to show the government that there is a need for exploration in the new settlement and to request financial aid. • Do not review the reasons for exploration as this is an evaluation activity.	• Did writing demonstrate —appropriate format for report? —appropriate features of a governor's writing in that period (empathy)? • Did writing identify appropriate and accurate reasons for needing to explore in the new colony? • Was the report written appropriately for —its audience —its purpose?
		RESOURCES
		• Examples of governors' reports from the first settlement.

Example 1 shows how children might learn through reading and writing a variety of text types. Not only would children involved in this unit learn the Social Studies content through these activities, but also their general reading and writing skills would be improved through their exposure to and engagement with creating numerous texts which organize information for different purposes. Such experience furthers the children's learning in all subject areas, not just in Social Studies. A similar trend can be identified in Example 2.

Example 2 **Science/Literature**

Purpose of Unit: children will conduct a study of animal behaviour and develop specific skills and knowledge through researching spiders.

The unit also serves to widen children's recreational reading and writing experiences by placing E. B. White's novel, *Charlotte's Web*, at its centre.

FLOW CHART OF UNIT

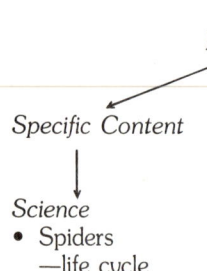

Specific Content

Science
- Spiders
  —life cycle
  —food
  —environment
  —behaviour

Language Arts
- E. B. White, *Charlotte's Web* (Puffin 1982)

Processes being Developed

- Finding information
- Identifying main ideas
- Sequencing
- Making inferences
- Critical thinking
- Hypothesizing
- Reporting
- Generalizing

Written Texts being Used/Developed
- Procedural
  —listing
  —graphing
  —note-taking
  —instructions
- Expository
  —reports
  —science books
  —reference books
- Narrative
  —fantasy fiction
  —animal stories
- Artistic
  —plays
  —poems

Application/Evaluation of Knowledge Acquired

- Write an expository book about spiders for a younger grade.
- Write and perform a play depicting an incident showing friendship.
- Write a report of an experiment conducted with a spider.
- Design an experiment to examine the behaviour of another animal when exposed to light, sound and changes in temperature.
- Write a description of a spider in narrative or artistic form.

Activity 1: Beginning of Unit
Purpose: to introduce the novel to the children and to provide a context for the unit; to identify a purpose for researching spiders, i.e. to find out more about Charlotte.

OBJECTIVES	STRATEGY	EVALUATION
General • Begin reading the novel and identify spiders as a research topic. *Specific* • Encourage attentive listening. • Discuss the beginning of the novel and predict outcomes. • Identify what children know and need to know about spiders. • Identify methods of research.	• Read and tell the first four chapters. • Ask children to predict the next chapter and give their reasons. • Discuss Charlotte. Children build a retrieval chart showing what they know and don't know about spiders. • Through discussion identify methods of finding out information. Focus on —people —materials —experiments —spiders' activities. • Collaboratively plan some activities.	• Were children's predictions logical and well reasoned? • Did predictions show evidence of attentive listening? • Examine chart for children's knowledge. • Plan/adapt future lessons on the basis of discussion about research.
		RESOURCES
		• E. B. White, *Charlotte's Web* (Puffin 1982). • Materials for chart.

Activity 2: Middle of Unit
Purpose: this activity has purpose in both Science and Language Arts. It helps children refine their skills in conducting an experiment, and in hypothesizing, inferring and drawing conclusions. These cognitive processes are developed further in a language activity requiring children to write a report on the experiment—introducing them to the demands of writing and reading text to satisfy a particular purpose.

OBJECTIVES	STRATEGY	EVALUATION
General • Conduct an experiment. *Specific* • Hypothesize results of the experiment orally. • Make inferences based on results. • Write a report of the experiment.	• Outline the procedures for conducting an experiment examining a spider's reactions to light, sound, heat and cold. • Assign children to groups to conduct the experiment. • Ask children to share results and lead discussion so that they make inferences about the spider's behaviour. • Review method of writing a report —structure/purpose —expression. • Examine examples of reports. • Ask children to write a report of the experiment.	• Did children conduct experiments —carefully? —accurately? • What was the quality of their —hypotheses? —inferences? • Were they well reasoned? • Were their reports —correctly set out? —clearly expressed? —accurate?
		RESOURCES
		• Appropriate for experiment. • Examples of good and bad reports.

Activity 3: End of Unit
Purpose: this activity is related more to the Language Arts strand of the unit. Part of an evaluation activity, it will in some ways assess the children's understanding of the friendship theme in *Charlotte's Web*. It will also develop their knowledge of another text type by engaging them in writing.

OBJECTIVES	STRATEGY	EVALUATION
General • Write a play. • Perform a play. *Specific* • Identify the theme of *Charlotte's Web*. • Discuss ways in which friendship can be demonstrated. • Revise format for play-writing.	• Discuss the theme of *Charlotte's Web*. • Discuss ways in which friendship can be demonstrated. • Ask children to relate relevant incidents in their life. • Review play-script conventions. • As a class select an incident from those the children related. • Negotiate the writing of a class play depicting that incident over the next few days.	• How easily did children identify the theme? • Did incidents the children related show understanding of the theme? • Did children's contributions to the play indicate —understanding of the play-script format? —understanding of the friendship theme?
		RESOURCES
		• Materials for class play-writing. • *Charlotte's Web*.

Planning and organizational implications

Integration of content, language and thinking has been long talked about, but attempts to forge connections between them have focused mostly on designing cross-curriculum activities around a common theme or topic. The units of work provided as examples here show a different and possibly more effective way of integrating them—through planned, modelled and varied writing and reading activity. Through writing and reading to learn, subject 'barriers' are withdrawn. The science/literature example shows this effectively.

If one does use such an integrative approach, however, what are the planning and organizational implications? They can best be summarized as two principles.

1. *Organization is essential.*

It is imperative that units be organized to ensure that all content and process objectives are achieved. Too often one becomes excited about the planned activities themselves, which results in the unit's objectives being lost in a sea of 'fun' or 'interest'. Each illustration provided in this chapter has clearly defined objectives correlating with the unit's overall purpose. If each time an activity is planned a comprehensive flow chart maps its development and purpose, then its scope and sequence should be logical and well balanced.

Interactive modelling of text refines understanding.

2. *A balance of text types should be maintained.*
Earlier in this chapter a range of text types and their intentions was outlined. To ensure balance in any reading and writing to learn program, one should constantly refer to such a range. Not only should one check that a variety of text types is being encountered, but that they are continually being modelled, revised, re-introduced and refined as they arise naturally for different purposes and audiences. It is as pointless for children to write a report in one unit and never write a report again, as to assume that children will know all about reports, their structure and purposes on the strength of one example. To ensure that they come to know the full range of text types, they must be re-introduced to them frequently both through reading and writing.

Conclusion

This chapter has explored aspects of the interrelatedness of reading, writing and learning. By way of illustrated curriculum units employing a variety of texts, it has drawn attention to our task of helping children interact intentionally with text to achieve learning outcomes. We need now to seek out varied texts of good quality which will help us realize those objectives.

5 Thinking-through Text

Bert Morris
Brisbane College of Advanced Education

Literacy teaching in the upper primary school has suffered from a lack of direction over the years. Although the content of various subject areas is outlined in curriculum guidelines, there is no universal agreement as to what should be taught under the rubric of 'reading' or 'writing' beyond the early years of schooling. Whereas we have been fairly clear on the objectives of beginning literacy teaching, that has not often been the case beyond Year Three. It is thus difficult for teachers to determine children's literacy development through the whole period of schooling, since criteria for evaluation and assessment cannot be established without specified goals. While such a situation may be reprehensible, teachers and schools are hardly to blame. School reading curricula can only reflect what is 'known' by theorists and researchers, and until fairly recently the whole field has lacked direction.

Following the work of Goodman (1967) and Smith (1971), the 1970s saw the rapid acceptance of a psycholinguistic theory of reading. The days of the 'Great Debate' of the mid-1960s between proponents of the phonic and whole word methods of teaching beginning reading seemed remote, and the issues ill-conceived. During the 1970s several other movements emerged, adding to the pyschologuistic perspectives sweeping the field. First came the Content Area Reading insights provided by Herber (1970), Robinson (1975) and others. These workers showed that literacy was a relative phenomenon. One might be highly literate in Physics but not in Law. Herber and his followers demanded that children be taught the skills required to read content area texts, not by specialist reading teachers but by subject area teachers. Reading thus came to be seen as a developmental process which needed assistance at all levels of primary and secondary schooling.

In the United Kingdom, Dixon (1975), Britton et al. (1975), Barnes (1976), Martin et al. (1976) and others showed that writing facility also developed slowly over time. They showed that content area teachers in secondary schools could greatly encourage this development by varying the purposes for which writing was used, and by providing students with different roles and audiences for writing in different forms.

Towards the end of the 1970s, linguists and cognitive psychologists began to make important contributions to the field as they started to examine the nature of larger sections of text and the processes we use to understand them. Their insights now allow us to look at ways of reforming curricula and to aim at providing students with the means for learning—not just with a body of factual knowledge which is being rapidly outdated.

Our aim in the upper primary school should be to ensure that children can process written text in a wide range of contexts. This includes writing their own texts, to help them learn as they write and develop their ability to convey their thoughts and understandings to others as clearly and logically as possible.

Traditional approaches to literacy teaching

In 1978 Dolores Durkin published evidence which showed that little, if any, attempt was made in United States primary schools to teach comprehension. What usually happened was that teachers tested to see whether children could answer questions about a piece of written text. These questions were usually of a literal nature, focusing on details provided in the text: 'How big was . . .? How old is . . .? Who said . . .? Where was she going . . .?' and so on. Answers were stipulated. You either found the correct answer or you didn't. Little attempt was made to teach children how inferences or conclusions could be drawn from the information given, or how ideas could be interpreted from different points of view. Comprehension was by and large tested, not taught. Durkin's findings have not been challenged and are widely accepted as being an accurate description of what happens in many classrooms even today. In Britain, Lunzer and Gardner (1979) showed that neither did secondary teachers do much to help students develop literacy skills. In lengthy observations of class teaching, they found that teachers rarely asked students to take time to think about the meaning of written texts. Instead, reading tasks were typically short, guided searches for an answer to a literal question.

Chapman (1983) found that few British primary schools taught reading skills across the curriculum. Thus, when children arrived at secondary school, Chapman found they suffered from what he termed 'register shock'. That is, they were not familiar with the language and style of the text books used in subjects such as Science or History, and their progress was frequently impaired as a result. This view is supported by Caffee and Curley (1984), who believe also that 'many youngsters fail to make the step from primer to textbook . . . partly because of a lack of conceptual clarity in the curriculum' (p. 162).

Informal enquiries I have made when giving workshops in primary schools suggest that both Durkin's and Chapman's findings apply to many of the Australian teaching situations with which I have come into contact. Few teachers attempt to show children how comprehension is achieved, and little or no attempt is made to teach children how to apply literacy skills across the curriculum. Thus, comprehension is still tested rather than taught, and subject area reading and writing too often focus on rote learning and copying of content. These are harsh words, perhaps, but if you don't believe them, ask some teachers how they teach literacy skills. On the basis of my experience, I believe you would find that schools do not teach literacy skills as *applied* skills systematically across the curriculum.

Process writing

One bright change in recent years has been the advent of the 'process writing movement'. Although the nature and intentions of teaching process writing have been

misunderstood by some, a lot of fine work has been achieved by others. The benefits of this movement to my mind have been:
- that teachers have started to respond to what children say and are now encouraging the growth of clear, personal expression
- that writing is beginning to be seen as a developmental process which goes through a series of stages.

Whilst progress has been made by the process writing movement, many teachers remain to be convinced that writing is a learning experience which helps the writer marshal and clarify ideas. Too many people unfortunately see it as a one-off method of assessing the level of a student's performance or knowledge.

What traditional teaching practices seem to reflect is an orientation towards the learning of content rather than an orientation towards the development of thinking and understanding. Courtney (1984) suggests that in many cases expository methods of teaching are enforced by teachers' striving to produce test results which prove that their pupils have 'learnt' in school. The facts and styles they have 'learnt' will, Courtney suggests, subvert attitudes to real learning. This view is supported by McGaw and Lawrence (1984), who note that much educational practice relies on the use of repetitive exercises rather than the development of problem-solving skills. The remainder of this chapter will suggest a number of ways in which we can help develop thinking and understanding.

Teaching children to apply reading skills in different reading contexts

It is imperative that we view literacy as a series of accomplishments which are applied in a variety of reading and writing contexts. This means that we cannot teach children literacy concepts using, say, science texts and believe that we have given them the concepts necessary for dealing with stories or poetry. Literacy concepts simply do not transfer readily from one context to another. This is true of adults as well as children (Lawrence, Dodds, Volet and Browne 1984). If we are to familiarize children with the features of texts used in Science or Mathematics or Social Studies or English/Language Arts, then we need to let them gain this familiarity by having them read, discuss and write the kinds of language registers and genres which are used in those areas. We must teach children how to get at, or present, information in different curriculum contexts. Just as they need to be taught how to process science or social studies materials, so too do they need to be shown *strategies* which will help them deal with genres such as stories, poems and plays.

Teaching literacy skills through narratives helps children deal with narrative text, but whilst this is a worthwhile objective in itself, it does not resolve the question of how children can be helped to write or read text in other contexts which demand science reports, explanations of how to solve maths problems, instructions on how to read maps, or accounts of the reasons for historical events. We need to realize that the language and type of information demands made by these different purposes require the use of different thinking and literacy skills. Using text material in a range of genres will provide children with a variety of reading experiences and allow teachers to teach appropriate processing techniques as they are needed.

It is important to realize what this implies. Not only should teachers provide practice and instruction using a range of reading materials, they should also see this to be a main function of their teaching. I do not believe that this is the case at the moment. Very few teachers in my experience realize that in the upper primary school one of their main responsibilities should be to teach language as an applied skill—that is, the use of language in different contexts for different (but real) purposes. Thus we should be teaching children 'how to' read science books, history books and so on; 'how to' write in styles appropriate to Science, History and other subject areas for varied purposes.

Developing more direct teaching towards specific aims

If we accept the need to teach literacy in a range of contexts, we have to look at how this can be achieved. Although in recent years reading schemes such as Mount Gravatt, Young Australia, Reading Rigby and Expressways have given teachers access to reading materials from different content areas, which introduce children to text varieties across the curriculum, the question still remains, 'What will we do with these materials?' For the fact is that any materials are only as good as the teacher's use of them. Unless teachers set out to teach children how to deal with the differing demands of different texts, many children will do no more than gain a passing acquaintance with these resources. Whilst this may provide useful experience, its value can be much greater if children are given intensive, text-based practice aimed at developing confident, strategy-based learning with long-term benefits in mind. Consider the following example.

> Karl and Matilda could clearly remember the morning Ottar's little knorr had sailed. They had helped load the boat with food for the seafarers: salt-meat, smoked fish, grain, butter and cheese, nuts and fruit, barrels of beer and fresh water. There were also goods which would be needed in faraway settlements, such as iron, timber, grain and salt, and a few luxuries such as jewellery and ornaments, which they hoped to trade. They would trade these goods for oils, furs and hides, sea ivory, and ropes made from walrus leather. Karl and Matilda longed for their father to return. He would not only bring news and stories of Iceland—but he might also bring his family presents of walrus ivory or furs. The year was AD 982.

(From *Explorers*, Reading to Learn Series, Longman Cheshire, in press)

As teachers we could use this piece of text in several ways. We could use it for oral reading practice; we could look at the setting it implies—a busy jetty with a small ship being prepared for a long voyage; we could focus on the children and their father and wonder about their feelings as they prepare for a long separation, or we could focus on the various lists of commodities presented. If we were to examine the setting or the kinds of feelings the people might be experiencing, we would be concerned to develop the kinds of skills associated with the study of English/Language Arts; on the other hand, if we were to focus on the lists, we would be concerned to develop skills more frequently used in subjects such as History or Social Studies.

Let us look at some of the tasks involved if we focus on the lists provided in the text.

Food for the seafarers	*Goods needed in faraway places*	*Luxury goods to trade*	*Goods obtained by trading*	*Presents*
salt-meat	iron	jewellery	oils	walrus ivory
smoked fish	timber	ornaments	furs	furs
grain	grain		hides	
butter	salt		sea ivory	
cheese			walrus-leather ropes	
nuts				
fruit				
barrels of beer				
fresh water				

The several lists present in the text have been extracted and organized under headings also taken from the text. They are the headings that children are likely to select. Although the construction of such lists seems to be a fairly straightforward task, several steps are involved.

Firstly, the reader has to *recognize* that several different lists are embedded in the text. Secondly, the information needs to be *sorted* into sets of related items. Thirdly, the sets of items require labels or headings. This means that the reader has to *identify* what the listed items have in common and find or invent a general label to act as a heading.

During this construction process, a number of questions have to be answered. For example, is the food to be used entirely on the boat during the voyage? The implication from the text is that it is: why else would grain be listed twice? Why is salt placed in the 'goods needed in faraway places' list and not in the food list? Further down, does the text imply that both the 'goods needed' and the 'luxury goods' are to be traded? (I believe it does.) Finally, can we infer that all the 'goods obtained by trading'—oils, furs, hides, sea ivory and walrus-leather ropes—are to be brought home? The text is not absolutely clear on this point, only mentioning the possibility of walrus ivory and furs being brought home as presents. (Is walrus ivory the same thing as sea ivory?)

Compare this kind of in-depth examination of the passage with its use as a practice piece for oral reading. To carry out an analysis of the text the reader has to recognize that several lists are involved; has to form generalizations to make headings; has to determine whether items should be placed in more than one list. Such activity, I would suggest, has long-term benefits applicable to many forms of text. Readers do need to be able to *extract* the different ideas which texts convey, and they do need to be able to *organize* these ideas in a way which enables them to make use of the information (Morris and Stewart-Dore 1984). As we can see from the example above, providing wider literacy experience is not enough in itself. We need to use print resources analytically, trying all the time to show children how to get at the information they need (Brown 1982; McGaw and Lawrence 1984). Such explicit teaching is only possible if we carefully examine what it is we want to teach and relate to this our increasing knowledge of how people learn.

For example, suppose we want to use a range of resources to teach children how to take notes or to summarize. A set of recently published workbooks purporting to teach children how to think includes a number of exercises on summarizing with this instruction: 'Pick out the main points and write a sentence about each one. This will give you a summary of the passage.' No help in identifying the main points is given; children are simply expected to do it. No instructions are given to the teacher, nor are children urged to share their ideas and justify why they think the points they have selected are particularly important. Presumably the work will be corrected in many classes on a right-wrong basis. Certainly the texts do not encourage the consideration of alternative answers. This is an example of traditional teaching which tests rather than teaches.

What can be done if we explicitly want to teach note-taking or summarizing? First, we should recognize that novices find it difficult to distinguish between important and unimportant information when they are dealing with unfamiliar ideas. A summarizing exercise will always be difficult for people who are unfamiliar with the content. Thus, such an exercise should awlays be preceded by work designed to familiarize the child with the topic. Second, we should recognize that many children find it difficult to pick out main ideas from details. Brown (1982) has shown that this is a skill which develops gradually and is considerably affected by the complexity

Distinguishing main ideas and supporting details is basic to summarizing information.

of the prose being read. She found that whilst children as young as six could identify main characters and events in a *single* story, children of ten could distinguish only the most important elements of a *more complex* story. However, with help in focusing their attention on what to look for, children could identify main features (Baker and Brown 1984).

Summarizing needs to be understood initially as an analysing exercise which involves distinguishing between main ideas and details and identifying any irrelevances which can be discounted. Systematic preparation of summaries cannot even begin until these skills have been developed. Teaching summarization should therefore start by helping children sort information into more and less important sets in order to develop the concept of hierarchical relationships. One would expect that children who can do this will be better able to distinguish main ideas from supporting details than children who cannot. A developmental sequence might be devised as follows.

(a) Exercises involving sorting, e.g.

Which things go together?

   dog, apple, cat, donkey, food, bread, animal

How many sets does this give you? How are they alike? How are they different? (Incidentally, this is the kind of thinking involved in making comparisons and contrasts.)

(b) Exercises in which information can be visually organized into map-like or chart structures, e.g.

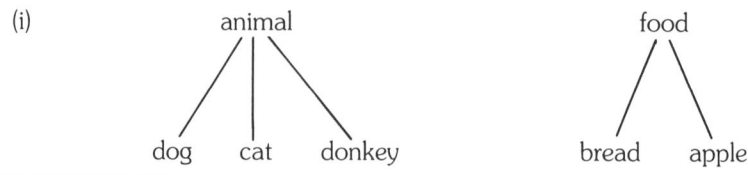

(ii)

animal	food
dog cat donkey	apple bread

Although the original information was given as a list of words in this example, children frequently encounter prose passages which contain similar sequences of ideas—for instance:

> John lived on a farm and helped his father look after the goats, pigs, sheep and cows which they kept. He enjoyed doing this but did not like to have to go out working in the paddocks where his father grew wheat, sunflowers, and sorghum.

This passage can also be analysed and organized into either a tree diagram or a retrieval chart.

(i) Tree diagram

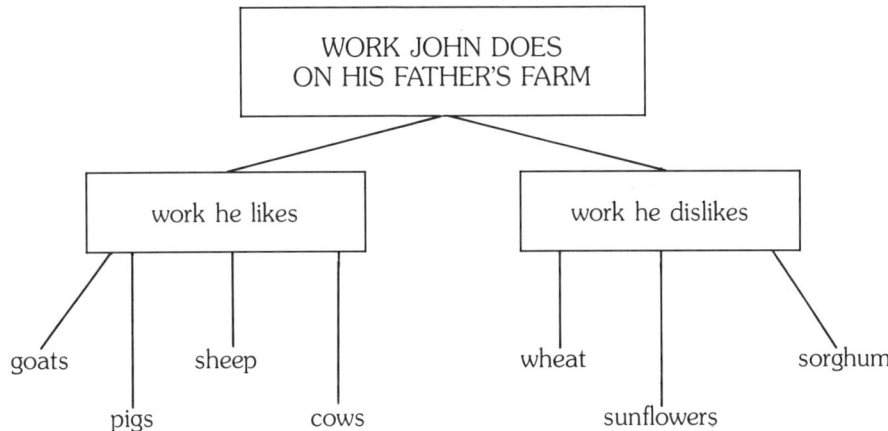

(ii) Retrieval chart

WORK JOHN DOES ON HIS FATHER'S FARM	
work he likes	work he dislikes
goats sheep pigs cows	wheat sunflowers sorghum

In both diagram and chart, headings have been used to group the two sets into 'Work he likes' and 'Work he dislikes', and a third heading has combined these into 'Work John does on his father's farm'. A similar approach could be taken to note-taking (which I see as a skill that develops before summarizing). Information about the farm might be set out in note-form like this:

(iii) Note-form

Products of John's father's farm

A Animals
  1. goats
  2. pigs
  3. sheep
  4. cows.

B Crops
  1. wheat
  2. sunflowers
  3. sorghum.

Finally, the passage could be summarized as:

John lived on a farm and enjoyed helping his father with the animals but not the crops.

Here the list of goats, pigs, sheep and cows has been grouped under the superordinate term 'animals', whilst wheat, sunflowers and sorghum have been placed under the collective term 'crops'. This method of teaching the use of superordinates is given by Day and Brown (1980), who provide the following list of rules for summarizing.

1. Delete unimportant information.
2. Delete redundant information.
3. Superordinate (use a superordinate in place of a list).
4. Iterate (select a topic sentence from the text and put into the summary).
5. Invent (not all paragraphs have topic sentences; some have to be made up for use in a summary).

From a teaching point of view, therefore, I think we have to start by looking at the processes we use when we try to carry out tasks such as summarizing. This kind of approach gives us something to work from, which must be a big improvement on just shaking our heads and complaining that 'kids can't summarize'.

Recognizing or imposing organization

Another systematic way to teach children to analyse text is to show them how to look for logical patterns or structures the author has used. These Organisational Patterns (Herber 1970) or Top-Level Structures (Meyer 1975) are found in many texts, and give us a way of showing children how ideas in text can be analysed. Besides patterns which the author has provided, we can also impose patterns of our own, which allow us to reorganize ideas from text to suit our own purposes.

The patterns commonly identified are:

Listing
Comparison-contrast
Elaboration
Cause-effect
Problem-solution

We have dealt with Listing earlier in the chapter, and most teachers are aware of the other names because they probably use exercises from different sources which purport to teach them. In my experience, however, very few of these exercises actually teach children *how* to recognize the different patterns; they only test recognition.

Comparison-contrast

You will recall that in the previous section on summarizing, the short passage about John was changed into this retrieval chart:

WORK JOHN DOES ON HIS FATHER'S FARM	
work he likes	work he dislikes
goats sheep pigs cows	wheat sunflowers sorghum

The original passage is an example of a comparison-contrast text structure. Notice, however, that none of the key words associated with comparison-contrast relationships (viz. in contrast, on the other hand, however, not only) are used to indicate this. The reader has to work out that likes and dislikes are being compared and contrasted. The retrieval chart gives a way of showing children this pattern, clearly dividing the items to be compared and contrasted into columns. We can alert children to this pattern by drawing up retrieval charts on the board when we come across a suitable piece of text, asking them to help us decide what lists of characteristics we should use.

Elaboration

A pattern of elaboration is characterized by a main idea followed by details which elaborate on it. For example:

> 'I like working in Mount Isa. The climate is warm and dry, the people are friendly, the motel meals are good and the pay is excellent.'

This becomes:
1. I like working in Mount Isa
   (a) the climate is warm and dry
   (b) the people are friendly
   (c) the motel meals are good
   (d) the pay is excellent.

Thus the basis for the pattern is:
1. main idea
   (a) supporting detail
   (b) supporting detail
   (c) supporting detail
   (d) supporting detail.

Cause-effect and problem-solution

The patterns of cause-effect and problem-solution are found in both narrative and expository text, and can be displayed in the format below.

Causes (or problems)	Effects (or solutions)
1 _____	1 _____
2 _____	2 _____
3 _____	3 _____

For example, in M. Thorpe-Clark's story *Joey* (1980), a mother is faced with a number of problems. Instead of just reading through the story and answering questions about it, children can be shown explicitly how to set out these problems and solutions in a retrieval chart like this.

PROBLEMS	SOLUTIONS
1 Her son wants her to stop the car to help an injured kangaroo.	
2 Her son wants to care for an orphaned baby kangaroo, 'Joey'.	
3 She has to find out how to care for a joey.	
4 She has to find a makeshift 'pouch' for Joey to sleep in.	
5 Her landlord will not let her keep Joey in her flat.	

Explicit analysis of text using visual displays to show how ideas are organized needs to be repeated frequently in as many different contexts as possible. Curiously, very few adults have ever been taught to extract and organize information in this way, and they are often just as pleased as children are when they see this simple way of displaying it. If you are not familiar with the technique, it may take a little time to get to get used to it, but if you persevere you will soon learn to see how texts are, or can be, organized into one of these patterns.

As we have seen, the various kinds of text patterns suggest different display formats. Thus, comparison-contrast suggests a retrieval chart; problem-solution or cause-effect suggests a two-column layout, while a temporal sequence of ideas suggests a time-line. Other visual forms are possible: maps, flow charts, histograms, pie charts, graphs and so on.

Space does not permit me to provide further illustrations of these patterns, but I hope the examples given make the point. We should not be content to have children merely read orally through text, any more than we should set tasks which require children to process a lot of information internally. Instead we should be looking for ways to extract and organize information into visual displays which clearly and concisely present the ideas to be considered. The technique can be applied to narrative text just as well as to expository text, by using plot diagrams, semantic webs and story frames.

Carrying over to writing

Although so far we have only looked at examples of written text analysis, writers can employ similar strategies as they compose text. Children may first think of ideas they want to include in a particular piece, and then sort (classify) and organize them into a logical sequence before expanding upon them in draft writing.

In my experience, many students in secondary school write poorly because they do not pre-plan what they want to write about. Although expert writers may be able to construct text as they write, many novices are unable to do so. Thus, we get four-line paragraphs containing three or four good ideas which are not expanded. Too often, unfortunately, the teacher's comment is: 'Johnny can't write more than four lines.' However, if Johnny is shown how to record, say, one idea on each of a series of palm cards and then list related ideas underneath each key point, he can learn to expand his original four lines into more extended text. People like Johnny need the help of an 'external memory' or planner, such as palm cards, to show them how their ideas might be developed.

Teaching children to put ideas together

Another problem children have in reading is their inability to link ideas, particularly across sentences (Baker and Brown 1984). Reading word by word, some children fail to build up a meaning picture as they go. Although they are able to answer sentence level questions of the 'Who did what?' variety, providing these draw on their tacit knowledge of sentence structure (syntax), they are unable to interpret or combine ideas. Yet effective reading requires the reader to go beyond the single sentence and to join ideas across sentences. Take, for example, the following sentences, where the meaning is problematic.

Her bike fell down and the bell broke. Now she couldn't use it.

As we read, we ask ourselves what does 'it' refer to, the bell or the bike? Usually we would expect it to refer to the bell, the last subject introduced, but what if the passage proceeds like this?

Her bike fell down and the bell broke. Now she couldn't use it and would have to walk to school.

Would she have to walk to school if the bell were broken or is something more serious implied? Suppose there were regulations which said that only bikes with bells that worked could be ridden to school? The passage might now read like this.

Just before school ended, the teacher said, 'A policeman will be here tomorrow to check all bikes. Please make sure your bike is in working order if you do plan to bring it to school tomorrow.' Jane was up early next day and polished her bike till it shone. As she went in, her bike fell down and the bell broke. Now she couldn't use it and would have to walk to school.

In this context 'it' refers to the bike rather than the bell. But the information given is cumulative, and as readers we need to learn how to keep track of what is going on.

One effective way of teaching children how to build on information given in text as they read, rather than focusing on separate words, is to use cloze exercises. Not cloze tests, mind you, but cloze exercises.

A cloze test is a task in which you are (a) expected to provide the correct answer, and (b) will have to know the answer already because it is not given in the text. Teachers use cloze tests all the time to assess how much students know or have learned about a topic. See if you can complete this cloze test.

    I have _____ dollars in my wallet.

Any ideas? You might guess, but you don't 'know' the answer, do you? Compare that example with this one.

    I'll be _____ when payday _____ because I'm _____ and have not been able to pay the _____.

Any ideas this time? Readers can make a better attempt at completing this sentence because there are more clues provided. Which ones did you use? Try the sentence out on other people and see if they come up with the same words as you did. If you have different answers, try to work out why they are different and which are the most suitable. When you do try it out with others, you will begin to hear how people work out ideas. Such cloze exercises cause readers to read back and forth looking for clues in the text. Having children in small groups discuss possible solutions to deletions gives less successful readers the chance to hear how more successful readers 'read around' words to look for clues.

Try the cloze exercise that follows to see which clues you use in completing it and which blanks you can't fill because you can't find sufficient clues.

    Roads in the villages lead between high walls which _____ the private dwelling places of separate families. The _____ are made of reddish mud and are topped _____ a protective thatch of lantai grass. As a stranger walks through the village, _____ emerge from narrow gateways and bark unpleasantly. One dog alerts others until dogs are barking far _____ and far ahead of the _____ stranger.

    Also on a village road you might see _____ Balinese cattle with golden coats and large brown eyes, tethered out to graze. Or you _____ see a buffalo in the charge of a small boy, or a sway-back pig being led _____ a graceful girl. _____ of ducks waddle and _____ beside the road, followed by boys who carry bamboo poles.

                                             (Beath and Cox 1981, p. 7)

Using peer tutors

A resource we can make more use of is the children themselves—as teachers of other children. We do not as yet fully understand the learning process, and so we are not in a position to properly structure learning situations even if we want to. We do not know why some people *do* learn whilst others do not, even when their background and the teaching they have received appear to be identical. Increasingly, however, the difference between people who do seem to learn easily and those who don't is intriguing researchers (Bransford and Nitsch 1978; Brown 1981; McGaw and Lawrence 1984; Lawrence et al. 1984).

The aim of these researchers is to find out how experts manage to process and understand text, so that their methods can be taught to novices. One enormous difficulty is to identify what goes on in other people's heads, and one way is simply

Small group discussion of text clarifies ideas.

to ask them (Brown 1982; Rumelhart 1984). Such self-reports, either ongoing thinking aloud commentaries, or after-the-event thinking back accounts, are now frequently used by researchers such as Baker and Brown (1984) to try to get experts to reconstruct their thought processes. What has this to do with classrooms, you might ask?

The use of small, mixed-ability group discussions has long been recommended (Barnes 1976; Morris and Stewart-Dore 1984), and a description of how they can work to clarify and extend understanding is given by Jan Weis in Chapter 6. Such groups have been seen as a way of providing interpretations of text by more able for less able students. The more recent research focus on experts vs. novices now shows small groups in a new light. Originally recommended by Barnes as a way of developing language skills and thinking and of providing less able students with a risk-free environment in which to talk through problems, small groups can now be seen as providing opportunities for novices to *listen* to children who are more expert talking-through *the way they think*. Novices can be given immediate feedback on how a point here and a point there can be selected from a text to help someone more expert reach a conclusion. Moreover, the explanations provided will be in child-to-child terms rather than in a teacher's more formal subject language, which Britton et al. (1975) found to inhibit learning so much.

One outstanding benefit of small group discussions is that they improve motivation to learn by reading. This effect has been noted in secondary classes by Downing (1983) in Queensland and Penton (1985) in New Zealand. In both cases, a content area reading program, using planned activities which relied on small mixed-ability discussion groups, was shown to encourage novice learners to take an active part in classes in which they had previously found coping difficult. As a result of being more involved, these novices were highly motivated and produced much better work than before.

Use of such groups, however, does require the teacher to structure learning activities carefully. The teacher must analyse the tasks to be completed so that children can be guided in their progression from point to point (Applebee 1982; Baker and Brown 1984), and must ensure that activities *anticipate the thinking* that readers need to employ to complete tasks successfully.

Conclusion

In this chapter I have tried to show that reading and writing are thinking activities, and that we should concentrate much more than we do on making children think about how they can find the meaning in a variety of texts. Baker and Brown (1984), who have done much in recent years to help us understand how we learn through reading, draw attention to the need to make learners aware of *how they learn*. They have shown that students who are made to use study strategies such as making notes, or underlining, do not gain any long-term benefits until they start to incorporate these strategies spontaneously for themselves, signalling that they understand how and why they work. Thus, if we do adopt the kinds of activities discussed in this chapter, it is imperative that we try continually to get students to understand why we want them to use them. If we succeed, we will be well on the way to producing independent learners.

6 Writing and Reading to Learn Together

Jan Weis
Sunnybank Primary School

with

Nea Stewart-Dore

In 1983 I implemented a process approach to writing across the curriculum. This meant that instead of merely 'assigning' writing tasks, I had to show children how to meet the demands of differing writing tasks by becoming a writer myself. In the process I became more critically responsive to the kinds of problems that cropped up as children tried writing extended, cohesive texts for different purposes. I learned also to listen more closely to what children were telling me about their ideas, their language, their thinking, their texts.

During these encounters with what were, in fact, ways of thinking about the nature and variety of text, in which children made new meanings and posed questions to which I had few answers, I wondered how I could help them to transfer the skills they were adept at using in Language Arts and Library 'reading' sessions to situations which asked them to think about, understand and compose different kinds of text in Maths, Social Studies, Art, Science and Health.

My class work program listed linguistic and cognitive objectives for all curriculum areas. It 'said' all the right things about developing children's abilities to form concepts, see relationships among ideas, make inferences and draw conclusions, apply knowledge, solve problems, summarise information, sequence, structure, compare and contrast ideas, and see how authors organise text to make meaning. Yet these objectives didn't hang together, and my approach to teaching reading was no more successful in realizing them beyond Language Arts. This was especially apparent when we came to dealing with ideas in expository text. I needed to develop activities that connected reading explicitly with the writing we were doing within and across subject areas, so that children could develop their language and thinking processes to structure knowledge (i.e. learn content) in text.

What was going on in my classroom?

My teaching problem must have been a massive learning problem for my pupils, but I was not sure how to solve it. I knew that there were imbalances in my teaching program, but it's very difficult to analyse precisely what's going on when you are kept busy dealing with children's urgent questions. I needed a friendly critic to pinpoint for me the disparities between what I intended to do and what I was actually doing. So I invited Nea Stewart-Dore to investigate the literacy learning and teaching events in my classroom, and to determine how I might forge connections between what had become disparate and fragmented attempts to satisfy curriculum objectives beyond Language Arts.

After observation and discussion, we agreed that if I were to improve the quality of literacy learning in all curriculum areas, I needed to:

- analyse the demands of both reading and writing tasks, identifying the information and language processing skills needed to complete them successfully
- teach all children the skills and processes required for particular tasks and follow them through in group activities in various curriculum areas
- examine how knowledge is structured through language and teach the children how to explore, create and structure meaning through reading and writing a range of genres.

Proceeding to learn

Teachers rarely see others teach. Although I employed strategies to help children use language to think about what they read, I needed some demonstration of how these strategies were integrated in the learning process. I also needed to distance myself

Small group interaction generates new understandings.

they interacted with each other and with text, so that
ly was happening as they did so. Nea and I swapped
rved. My role was to search and re-search the literacy
ustained by oral language, as they occurred, and to
ould analyse the events to plan for my future teaching.
reading, thinking and learning systematically by
ves; and as the 'content' focus for the literacy learning
a Social Studies unit, *Economic Planning*, beginning
ants and needs'.

ng and thinking activities

nowledge and learning outcomes, and to share

izing and structuring information to show relation-

ate ideas and link them in a variety of ways.
nformation and sequence ideas to achieve cohesive

.., text to reflect on literal, inferred and generalized meanings.
- Justifying in small groups responses to statements derived from text passages and presented for debate.
- Self-questioning to solve individual problems in understanding a text.
- Challenging each other's thinking; questioning to clarify understanding.
- Abstracting main ideas and comparing them in small groups to negotiate a common set of key points.
- Recording ideas in small groups during discussion and sharing them across groups.
- Note-taking to show distinctions between main ideas and supporting details; summarizing ideas and justifying their inclusion or omission.
- Developing draft writing in response to information gleaned from text and discussion, for specific purposes and audiences, from various points of view and in forms appropriate to the occasion.

As we analysed what was required to learn through text, it became clear how each activity had to derive from and support the others. It was no use going off in one direction without thinking about the implications for literacy learning elsewhere.

While Nea taught, I mapped the unfolding events. What follows is a synthesis of activity undertaken jointly over a six-week period.

Getting to know each other

Although no stranger to the children, Nea began by engaging them in a 'getting to know each other' activity which served two purposes. Firstly, it helped her become familiar with the children's interests and activities beyond school; secondly, the product of the interaction was to become the basis for composing short autobiographies to include with any future writing we might publish. The children were introduced to a form of writing which they had frequently read but rarely composed for themselves— namely a pen portrait.

Pre-writing discussion explored the nature of the biographical details about authors given on book blurbs and dustjackets. Drawing on prior knowledge, the children talked over what information it is appropriate to include in a public advertisement of self, and how it is conventionally staged in print to inform a reading public about an author. Choices made in composing such text were explored by Nea modelling how to select pertinent personal details. The children were particularly interested in how she rejected trivial, if fascinating information about her 'life' as she wrote in demonstration. Afterwards the children drafted their own introductions as authors to their potential but as yet unknown readership.

Nea read and responded to each draft text in writing. Of each writer she asked a series of questions which sought to clarify and extend information contained in the drafts. To learn from being challenged about what they had written, the children needed to re-read their drafts critically and evaluate them in the light of the response each had received.

In subsequent lessons I extended the study of biographical text by contrasting first and third person accounts of experience. I read a range of extracts which showed how authors achieve particular effects through linguistic choice when writing about their own and other people's lives. Over time, the children shaped their own pen portraits, adding and deleting details and rearranging the information they chose to make public. Problems about what they meant were resolved before they turned to the generic structure of the text and the adoption of an appropriate register. Our aim was to help them understand how this genre worked and could be shaped to support and enhance extended publishing efforts in the future.

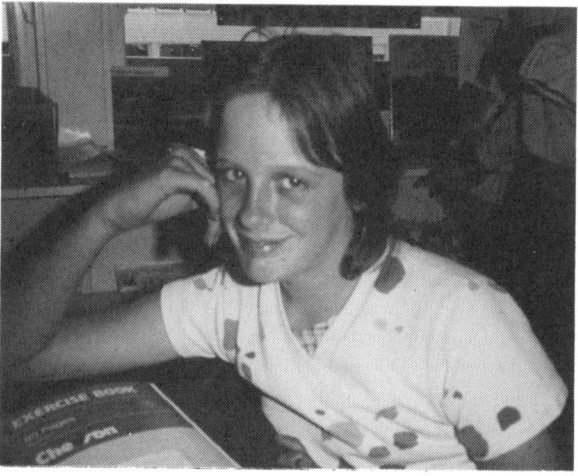

Sandra was born in Brisbane on the 18th of April 1973. She has a very big family consisting of one brother and three sisters. She has moved three times in one year and is now living at Holland Park a suburb of Brisbane. She attends Sunnybank State School. Her hobbies are collecting stickers and postcards from all over the world. Her favourite popstars are Michael Jackson and Bruce Springsteen. She also likes going to see movies such as Desperately Seeking Susan. Her only pet is a dog. She has entered a writing competition but she did not win anything.

Introducing the social studies topic

To introduce the contrasting concepts of 'wants and needs' we prepared the handout illustrated below.

Stranded

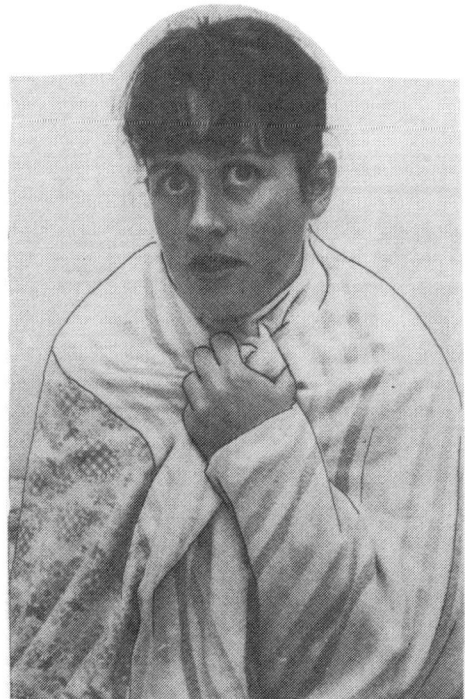

Peta saved hard to have a holiday in Australia. She planned to go to the Barrier Reef, but instead, she's stranded in Brisbane after losing her port containing all her clothes and personal belongings. Her money is running low as well.

If you were in her shoes, what would you be most worried about today?

Caption:

After some discussion, each pupil freewrote a response to the question posed. Small, mixed-ability groups were formed to share answers and negotiate group statements for scrutiny by the whole class. The children were placed in a situation where they had to recognize that other people's ideas demanded attention before they could reach and express a consensus view. They discovered how to arbitrate when conflicting views were presented and to rehearse and defend their own points of view.

The group opinions were recorded on a large sheet of butcher's paper. Worries were aired, commented upon, debated and discussed by the whole class. Decisions were made about which were the most urgent needs of the distressed person and these were ranked from most to least important. A significant feature of classroom discussion was the introduction of personal experience to support individual reasoning. Children drew naturally on prior knowledge to make connections with their daily lives—thinking, exploring, and taking risks to make meaning of the situation presented to them. I listened, fascinated by the range of analogies, comparisons and conclusions drawn as they made sense of the concept of 'need'.

When the children had reached agreement on the person's needs, a summary statement was formed and recorded on the blackboard. Since the objective was to form a *generalization* about needs, they were then invited to show how they would turn this specific statement into a generalization by making changes to the text. This generated considerable discussion about language itself, particularly about word choice and the grammar of sentences.

> We
> Peta needed food, clothing, accom. shelter
> health + our family support
> to { get rid of her worries.
>   survive.
>
> We need food, clothing, shelter,
> health and our family support
> to survive.

Developing concepts

To follow up the introductory lesson, I asked pupils to review what they thought they had learned by *recall freewriting*. Most expressed the concept of 'need' coherently before sharing their writing in groups. Some then modified their initial thinking by extending ideas contained in their freewriting.

We next *brainstormed* to *list* personal 'wants' before discussing how these might be *categorized* tentatively. We put headings on a large sheet of butcher's paper and added personal 'wants' under each one. Spontaneous debate arose over differences of meaning between categories such as 'Recreation' and 'Entertainment'. After viewing the extensive listing, the children concluded that: 'Even though we all have the same basic needs, our wants differ.' They were learning quickly to generate and apply thinking processes without my direction.

The refined category identification led naturally to the creation of a *structured overview*. This is what Morris in the previous chapter referred to as a *tree diagram*—

a hierarchical arrangement of ideas from the general to the specific. We had prepared a structured overview derived from the previous lesson in which 'needs' had been identified, and I used this to demonstrate to the children how to build one up for themselves. They argued heatedly over the meanings of words such as 'basic', 'nourishing' and 'healthy' foods, drawing on their knowledge of food groups studied in Health. Similar debate occurred over the meaning of 'shelter': did it include only regular dwellings, or might it extend to temporary, smaller units such as caravans or hotel rooms? Nicholas suggested that 'shelter' implied safety. The children then reflected on their lists of wants in groups. Having agreed finally upon the category headings, they drew up personal structured overviews and justified to each other their selection of items for each category.

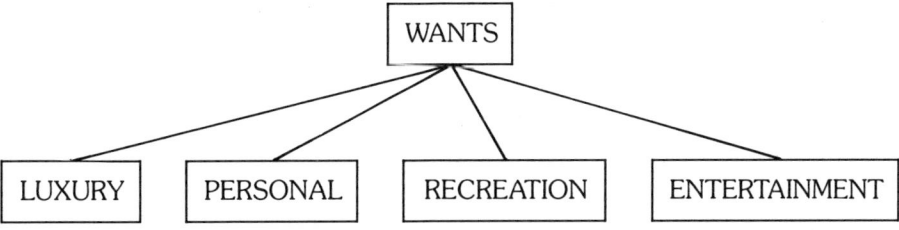

Then Nea posed the question: 'How are we going to satisfy our needs AND our wants?' To think through the problem, the children freewrote before point-form contributions were recorded on the blackboard, among them being the following:

- win Lotto/Casket
- money
- marry someone rich
- work for it
- inherit it.

Clearly the common element was 'money'. Greg concluded, 'We need money to buy our needs and our wants, so we have to go to work to get our money.' No one dissented and he asked, 'Can I draw what I mean?' This is his diagram:

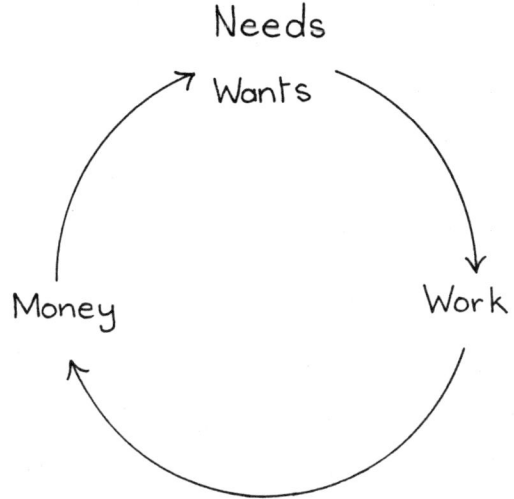

What excited me about the interaction was how these children so naturally took charge of their learning when challenged to do so. Observing the transfer of thinking from the teacher to the class was my most valuable lesson. Involving children in co-operative learning requires faith in their ability to reason, to use language purposefully, to question and to challenge; and it's not easy to throw off the remaining shackles of expository teaching. I could now see how it might be done.

Preparing to read expository text

The activities to date had prepared the children to 'meet the text', a formal presentation of information about wants and needs, economic planning and the manufacture and supply of goods and services. Together we had probed personal and vicarious experience, tapping prior knowledge, discussing ideas, recording them, reading them, reflecting on their import and selecting from them to organize and clarify how they related to each other.

To consolidate concepts so far discussed, we focused reflective thinking about a narrative text by designing a series of statements about its content. The children's task was to read the text *and* the statements, and in groups to decide and justify which statements

(a) were explicitly stated in the text
(b) could be inferred from the text
(c) might be applications of the main idea in situations outside the text.

The reflective reading required of the children proved difficult. Unused to re-reading text to question their personal responses to it, many were puzzled by there being no right or wrong answers. Others were mystified by being asked to explain *why* they chose particular responses. Although I often asked children to give reasons for their answers to questions about text in 'reading lessons', I did not always pursue these beyond simple articulation. What was different here was that as the children were being drawn into clarifying the text and their interpretation of it, they were challenging each other to make meaning. 'Where does it say that? *How* do you know that's true? It says here that ... now *how* do you explain that? But you haven't said *why* you agree with the statement. How do you *know* that's what the author means? I don't follow you ... what do you mean ...?' were typical exchanges.

I'd long been concerned about children's apparent difficulty in locating information in resource material, especially during library research tasks. What I needed was a system for teaching the efficient use of resource books.

Nea demonstrated how to survey using headings or 'signposts' to map sections of expository text. Using a prepared *graphic outline* displayed on an overhead projector, she referred the children to the text and showed them how to select the information needed to fill in the outline. After they had completed the task individually, their efforts were compared and a review session recorded observations about the nature of headings, sub-headings, details and examples, illustrations and captions. A freewriting exercise, completed in what was known as the pupils' 'learning log', checked their understanding of the nature and function of text signposts in a lesson the following day.

Adam

I learnt that sign posts are not only street signs but a way to find out a fast way to read a text book. I think I learnt alot today about signposts.

> Louise
>
> Signposts in reading can be headings, & illustrations sub headings so you can find the information your looking for a lot quicker. They direct us to where our information will be instead of having to read the hole book.

Confirming and modifying prior knowledge

Having surveyed the text, we used headings and sub-headings to frame *predictive questions* about its possible content. We then read to confirm or refute our predictions before reviewing our structured overview to modify its contents in the light of what we had read. We replaced, for example, some of our words like 'needs' and 'wants' with 'essential' and 'non-essential' respectively, and added details found in the text which we had not thought of previously.

Although this activity appears to be a simple one of comparing and contrasting information in the head with that in the book, the children had considerable difficulty in moving between the text and the structured overview. This, I think, was because the formal text language was remote from their experience, although they did understand the concepts that the language represented.

Applying information

We needed then to demonstrate how to extend and apply the understandings they had about 'wants and needs' or 'essential and non-essential goods'. To do this, we introduced them to the idea of a *word map*, which is a clustering technique to organize brainstorming ideas. I constructed a word map on the blackboard to demonstrate how ideas about 'community needs' could be generated and linked together. The children contributed ideas, drawing on general knowledge and information contained in the graphic outline. They were asked about the source of these ideas: were they 'in the head' or 'in the text'? The word map overleaf represents the outcome of the whole class effort.

Subsequently, each of six groups of children developed focused word maps from the web categories. They brainstormed, listed details for each concept and shared their maps, asking clarifying questions of each other. This in itself was interesting, because some selections were disputed by other groups and the word map designers had to justify their selection and rejection of detail. One group totally redesigned their effort when they realized that their concept of 'Transport' could be further subdivided into transport modes.

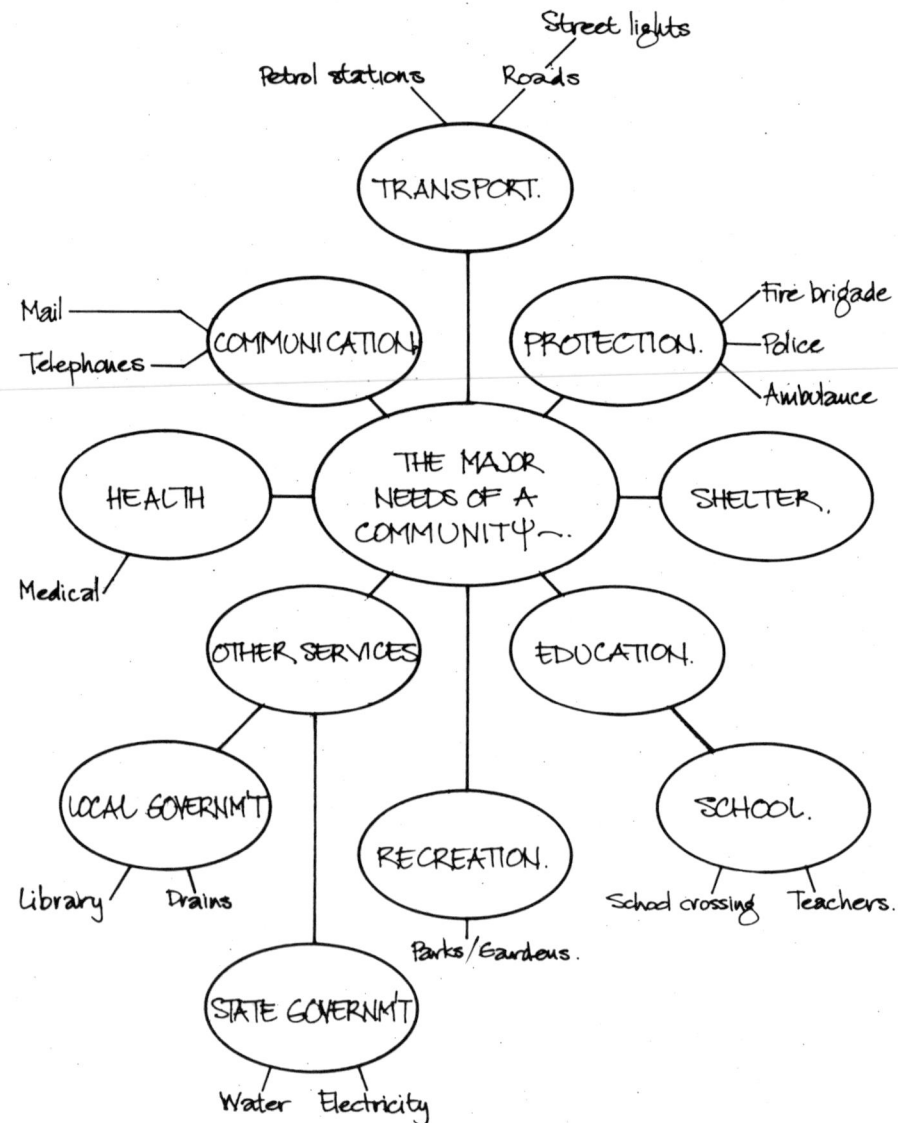

To conclude this activity, the children were asked to freewrite about what they thought they had learned. Here are some of their responses.

Lisa: Little things in the community are essential.
Stephanie: Services are linked to protection and to communication so people can contact each other. Health is also linked to transport because the ambulances have to go from place to place to accidents and then to hospitals.
Erika: The community need workers in everything. It links under all different headings on the blackboard. The most important thing is the workers to make everything work.

Nicholas: Most things make like a link in a long line of needs and just about everything needs the services to help each other along.
Greg: I've learnt that a community needs more than an individual.
David: A community as a whole needs to co-operate to get things done.

Clearly, the children showed that they were making connections among ideas. Through explicit reference to prior knowledge, negotiating ideas gained from reading, discussion and debate, sharing, comparing and contrasting them, 'mapping' to organize them systematically and writing to explain what they had learnt, they were showing me how literacy, thinking and learning are inseparable.

Extracting and organizing information

In the previous chapter, Bert Morris explained the importance of teaching children how to identify key points, sort out details and arrange ideas according to the author's top level structure. Where that has to be inferred, he suggested teaching children how to impose a pattern of organization on a text from which we want children to learn. I have described activities which derive from some of the ideas he discussed: for example, the use of word maps and structured overviews to organize ideas children offered in brainstorming sessions. Similarly, when reading narrative text, we have used story frames and semantic webs to help us make predictions and chart relationships among events and characters.

In preparing to teach the children how to identify, sequence and diagram steps in the process of producing, marketing and distributing goods, we guided them to list the steps outlined in the text. Most were stated explicitly, and so to avoid 'copying' we asked the children to reason and show how they knew a piece of information should be included as a step in the process. Where necessary, they were also asked to infer who would be responsible for various tasks or where the activity would be carried out.

A retrieval chart helped them with this task. I showed them an example of how it might be completed by 'thinking aloud' as I went from chart to text and back to the chart again to select, infer and record relevant points.

List of steps in . . . .

STEP	CLUE (if given)	PERSON/PLACE

When the time came for the children to compare and contrast their completed charts, I discovered that many had difficulty identifying clues that helped them know that a particular step was involved. They wanted to focus on the step only. There was much discussion as well about how they might resolve problems of recording people mentioned in the text for whom there was no clearly identified function in a process.

We decided to transform the information extracted and sequenced into pictorial chains with explanatory captions. These were shared among members of each group who commented on similarities and differences between them. Collectively, they were used to elicit generalizations about the three processes described. While some represented the process in more abstract flow diagrams, Adam's Production Process Chain looked like this.

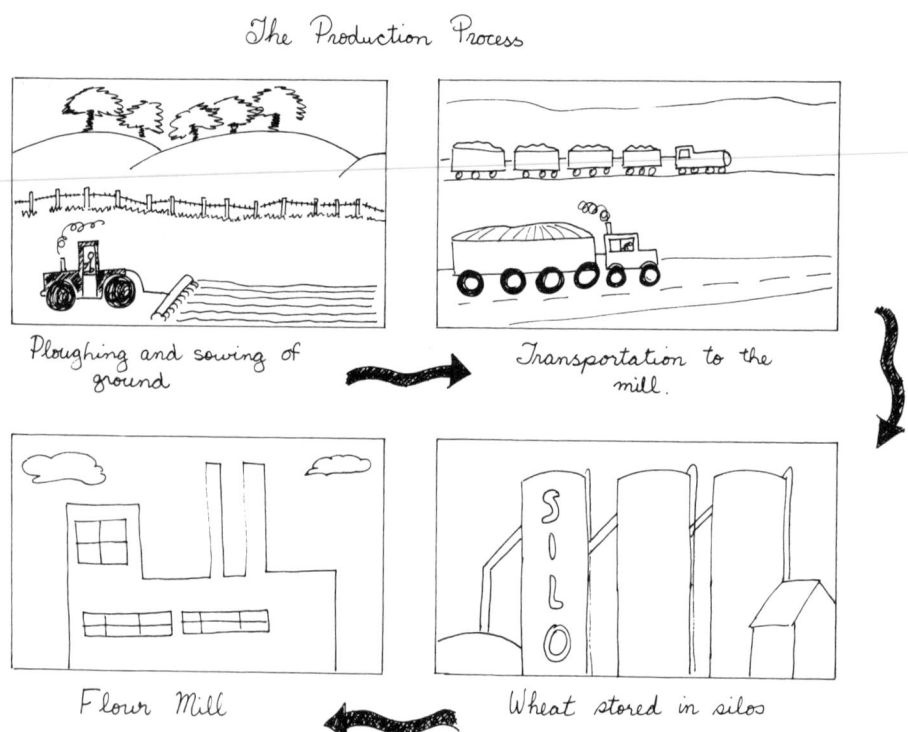

Writing as experts and novices

Having read and talked about, recorded and shared personal knowledge and information from the text source until we were thoroughly familiar with the major concepts of the Social Studies unit, our next task was to synthesize that knowledge and information into a purposeful piece of writing which could be shared with an audience other than ourselves. In the meantime, we had polished our personal pen portraits to include with any writing that we might publish.

First, however, we had to decide what we would write about. Earlier in the year, some children had exchanged with others from a rural school. The educational program had included visits to a pineapple farm, and to a preserving and canning factory. It was agreed unanimously that these experiences would provide the content for writing, using the now well practised strategies of pre-writing, drafting, responding, revising, editing, and proofreading to produce a polished piece.

Those who had not been involved in the visits would interview participants to gather information. This would help participants to recall and order ideas and focus their recollections. It also meant that no one would be disadvantaged, and since everyone know how to locate, reflect upon, extract, organize and synthesize information from text, specialist resource materials could be used to supplement and extend personal knowledge.

Our next task was to explore the possibilities for writing. We did this by using our now very familiar strategies to pool ideas and organize information—brainstorming and charting. We defined the context in which the writing was to assume meaning: the daily activities involved in farming, processing and canning pineapple. We talked about the people working, their tasks and the kinds of language exchanges that they would engage in as they went about their business. We rehearsed situations in which they might find themselves, exploring causes and effects through role play.

Finally we had to decide about the focus, perspective, purpose and audience for individual children's writing. Some of the possibilities we explored are outlined on the chart below.

CONTEXT	PURPOSE	ROLE	AUDIENCE	TEXT TYPE
RECALL OF VISIT TO PINEAPPLE FARM AND CANNERY	Imaginatively reconstruct production process	'Peter Pineapple'	Year 3 children	Picture story book
	Entertain	Self	Peers, parents	Poem, play
	Explain process	Farm worker	New employee	Dialogue script
	Guide visitors	Tour leader	Visitors to farm/cannery	Information pamphlet describing process
	Inform others	Newspaper journalist	Community	Feature article
	Comment	Narrator	Peers, parents, teachers	O.H.T.—tape documentary
	Record experience	Self	Peers	Learning log or journal

Naturally the process of gathering ideas, trialling them and shaping them into worthwhile text took time. At some stage or other I responded to all writing in progress. I wasn't 'swamped' by children clamouring for help with their emerging text, because each was dealing with a different kind of text which posed its own problems. Further, there was a range of abilities, and different children were at different stages in their drafting.

When children are engaged in extended writing tasks such as this, I have found them to be remarkably self-sufficient and happy to try to solve their composing problems for themselves, or to seek peer advice until I am available. As a particularly interesting problem arose, I would focus everyone's attention on it, demonstrating a decision-making or editing strategy by working from a child's draft. Issues of language choice, such as grammar or register, and problems with structuring text in a particular genre were dealt with in this way.

The written products were shared with parents at a special function the children arranged one morning towards the end of the year. They helped me to decorate the

Consulting text models for writing.

classroom with the accumulated artefacts of their learning processes: butcher-paper charts of exploratory thinking, summary statements, freewritten learning logs, diagrams and procedural guidelines for thinking through and making meaning of text by reading and writing. Although there were no award-winning children's stories, news reports or tourist brochures among their products, there was no doubt in my mind that their efforts represented the best of which they were capable at that point in their development.

Conclusion

Whereas previously I had separated writing and reading in Language Arts from writing and reading in other subject areas, I came to appreciate their power to make thinking explicit and to extend learning beyond subject 'boundaries'. While Nea and I were working with the children, I was conscious of the need to question how one activity which perhaps had a reading focus could lead naturally to a writing experience. It became increasingly clear that to write well one had to read critically. By learning how thoughtful reading could be fostered through talking about texts, I was able to see more clearly how to improve my writing teaching as well. What impressed me most was that both the children and I became more critical reviewers of our own knowledge, challenging not only what we found for ourselves, but also the very basis of how we knew what we thought we did know.

This collaborative effort merely started me on my learning and teaching journey. I know now that each year, as I begin working with a different group of children, they will teach me more than I yet know it is possible to know about literacy teaching and learning.

7 Writing and Reading Culturally

Nea Stewart-Dore

with assistance from

Rosemary Guttormsen
Queensland Department of Education

and

Nicki Kennedy
Provincial Newspapers (Qld) Ltd

Previous chapters have shown how children are socialized into writing and reading to learn from their earliest encounters with spoken and written language. Another focus has been on school curricula contexts and how teachers might help children make meaning by composing and comprehending a range of texts for different purposes. Implicit throughout is a definition of literacy as learned social behaviour. In this chapter, that definition of literacy is placed in the broader cultural context of our world.

When discussing those interactive language-using situations that occur in the home, the neighbourhood and the social facility of day care and pre-school, Parkes drew on features of our cultural environment to describe how opportunities to make sense of the world through print arise naturally. We expect children to achieve meaning through language, in both oral and written forms. Our culture reinforces that expectation through its demands for literate performance and its admonitions when schools appear to fail to ensure the mastery of 'popular' literacy.

Literacy culturally defined

Popularly, literacy is conceived narrowly. Perhaps that is why the view persists that literacy is an absolute to be measured in terms of children's ability or otherwise to 'read with comprehension', to 'spell accurately' and to 'use grammar correctly'. Narrowly conceived, literacy is narrowly 'taught'; narrowly taught, it becomes trivialized in its applications. Yet more liberal interpretations of what literacy can and does mean abound. A couple of examples will illustrate this, as we strive to interpret our individual and communal worlds.

Firstly, notions of literacy permeate our language. We use the words 'read' and 'write' in everyday speech to denote understandings of situations that bear little relationship to comprehending and composing written text. Thus, when we say in conversation, 'I read you', we signal our monitoring of meaning in the making; when police caution us to 'read the traffic' to avoid holiday congestion, we infer the need to delay, perhaps, our vacation departure; when politicians 'read the electorate' appropriately, they reasonably expect a further term of office; and when Australian cricketers 'misread the wicket' in Test matches against New Zealand, the outcome is a foregone conclusion.

Similarly, we may describe a person as having 'guilt written all over his face'; signal the need to bail out of a situation when 'the writing is on the wall'; and abandon an irreparably damaged object by 'writing it off'. In each instance, these words refer to our attempts to make sense of aspects of our world—our constant seeking to organize our perceptions of, thinking about and responses to it, to construct order and meaning.

Secondly, the term 'literacy' denotes ways of signing meaning in different fields. Such meanings or understandings include knowledge, skills and cognitive activity (which necessarily employ language) to define and organize thinking, action, attitudes and responses to perceived phenomena. Thus, computer literacy refers not only to awareness about and appreciation of the nature and uses of computers, but also to knowledge about and the skills required to generate, manipulate and control information in the technological world. Graphical literacy differentiates particular kinds of sign systems which organize the representation of thought through symbols, pictures, maps, graphs, diagrams and illustrations. In the social sciences there is concern to foster 'political literacy'. This involves the acquisition of propositional and procedural knowledge about, as well as critical awareness of, political systems and social agencies, and their relationship to the quality of citizen life.

Embracing all of these applications of literacy concepts is that of *cultural literacy*, defined by Boomer (1985, p. 10) as being able to 'read and write the world'. He suggests that teaching for cultural literacy in schools

> should lead students to even more subtle readings of the world and to even more accomplished, powerful acts, personally and in groups, intentionally designed to achieve purposes whether they be pragmatic, or aesthetic, personal or social.

Defining literacy culturally requires that we place 'text' within such a conceptual framework. In Chapter 3 Christie defined text to include both written and oral instances of language use, while Boomer (1985, p. 11) suggests that text embraces

> anything written or enacted or experienced which is *framed* in some way that makes it amenable to analysis and comprehension.

All texts, be they written, spoken, enacted or experienced, relate in special ways to the particular context which gives rise to their being. As we have seen, initial chapters explored specific home, neighbourhood and local community contexts which sponsor the need to learn to write and to read—to become literate in a traditional sense. Subsequent chapters examined how teachers can and do help children make sense of the many worlds that constitute school curriculum contexts. Each context delivers its unique texts to be written, to be read, to be enacted, to be experienced, to be understood and to facilitate understanding. To learn in any and all contexts, we need patterned sequences of experience and models of how to behave linguistically and cognitively through recursive journeys to textual places.

We now turn full circle to revisit the world beyond classrooms and books, which provides rich contexts for extending literacy and learning culturally.

Two products of our everyday world are computers and newspapers. They may be called 'cultural artefacts'—products, symbols and representations of what it means to live in our modern culture. To become culturally literate, children need to learn how to 'read and write' such artefacts, for they are among the many technological and media resources which frame our experience and hence our interpretation of the world.

Writing and reading computer technology as a cultural artefact

As adults, we may be bewildered by the role that computer technology increasingly plays in our lives. Such, however, is not the case with children. Learning about computers, their capabilities and operations to get things done, is a natural part of learning to read and write their everyday world. Julie is perhaps typical of her generation.

With her parents, 20-months-old Julie visited a friend's home. She was offered a croissant and her mother went to the microwave oven to heat it. As she did so, she said, 'Julie knows how to use ours at home. Come on, let's try this one.'

Whisked onto her mother's knee so that she could see and reach the control panel, Julie followed directions to activate the microwave oven.

'Now, first push the large button at the top. That's right. Now tell it how long to cook for. Push the 1 button. Now the large button at the bottom. Oh, it beeped at you. That's not the right button. Try the one beside it. That's right!'

The carousel began turning, heating Julie's croissant.

That negotiation provides an instance of socialization into the world of computer technology. Although it might be argued that Julie was merely following rehearsed behaviour, she was also engaged in learning how to write and to read a cultural artefact. As she was using and controlling a microwave oven under guidance, she was learning about the microwave oven itself, its role in a family routine, its operations and the associated language employed to get a task done. Specifically she was learning that computers

- need precise instructions in correct sequence before they will operate
- are controlled by users
- provide a form of feedback for operations
- are manipulable, as any action can be interrupted at any point and recommenced.

Computers are very much a part of Julie's everyday world. She watches her parents carry out financial transactions at automatic teller machines; she sees people entering, manipulating, reading and interpreting information at terminals in her father's office; she watches her parents, subscribers to Viatel, search for information from this large database. Throughout Julie demonstrates her curiosity, and her parents respond by inviting her participation in the processes involved. Always the interaction is supported by talk.

As a result of this interaction, Julie knows much about the meanings of numerous graphic symbols represented on the panels of machines and peripherals. Although unable to articulate these things, she knows that they convey meanings to be shared, negotiated, talked about, and acted upon. As a result of her encounters at home she will have little difficulty transferring these meanings to screen-reading knowledge on a personal computer at school.

Most children have many occasions for such computer literacy learning in their home and neighbourhood environments: by playing video, spatial matching or adventure games on home computers and on fun machines at leisure centres; by observing their parents use automatic teller machines; by seeing computerized databases in use in stores, businesses and public places such as airports. Many will use computer graphics, word processing, simulation games, and a range of computer peripherals, such as a mouse, joystick or pressure sensitive tablet, as alternative input devices in their everyday cultural encounters. In the process, children will learn how to mean technologically, interpreting the world through computers and extending their understanding of it.

Developing computer meanings

Computers in classrooms need to be seen as tools to *improve* learning in those areas where it is not possible to learn as efficiently or as effectively without them. In other words, computers should be seen as aids to get jobs done. Because not everyone is yet steeped in 'computer culture', however, we need to exercise caution in lauding computers' benefits. As Papert (1986), reported by Ives, maintains:

> I don't think the key issue is what kind of software there will be or what uses the computer will be put to, or even how the classroom is organised. The key process that will make the difference in the future is the growth of a culture around the computer, an integration of the computer into the general culture. The way that happens will determine what the computer can and cannot do.

Framing contemporary 'computer culture' are three principal functions of computers: word processing, database storage and retrieval, and spreadsheet presentation and display. Of these, word processing and database applications, as well as simulation and adventure games, offer greatest potential for integrating reading and writing to learn in the curriculum. Through their judicious use, it is possible to realize, in part, Boomer's definition of teaching for cultural literacy.

Word processing

The increasing use of word processors in schools means that most teachers are familiar with them to varying degrees. Even so, many have yet to use them as a personal instrument for composing and comprehending text and its structure, so that they may experience what their power means to children. Much has been written about word processors and their capacity to facilitate the writing process (e.g. Smith 1985; Wresch 1984). Research (Woods 1983; Stewart-Dore 1985) indicates that children who use word processors are highly motivated to write and revise extended text; they want to write more frequently than they do with traditional implements; they experience increased satisfaction with the quality of presented products, and they display a preparedness to share text during and after composition.

None of these benefits accrue, however, without close attention being paid to the nature and process of composing text. This is effected best through child-teacher collaboration, with the teacher demonstrating the kinds of relevant questions about text which will help the writer to solve problems of meaning and structure, thus encouraging revision beyond the correction of surface-level errors. Children need also to be shown how to reflect on text by assuming the role of reader to make predictions and inferences, so that they can link ideas logically throughout to realize coherent, cohesive pieces of extended writing. It is during this process of negotiating text that the reciprocity of composing and comprehending is most apparent.

Teachers employing word processors in teaching writing differ in their views as to the degree of keyboarding skill children need. Questions about typing skill and how word processor operations are best mastered, whether by drill exercises or while working on text itself, have yet to be answered. It is uncertain too how much knowledge is required about text composition processes (drafting, revising and editing) before using computers to facilitate writing. It will be some time before consensus is reached on these questions, or appropriate strategies refined to capitalize on the potential that computers offer in teaching writing.

Without doubt, however, the development of increasingly sophisticated word processing programs will affect the way we view and talk about text and its composition and comprehension in classrooms. For example, programs which empower children to present text visually for publication require decisions to be made about the amount and placement of text on pages. The integration of graphics to complement intended meaning, on the other hand, helps children to consider how comprehension may be enhanced by illustration. When children use creative software for story processing they generate new ways of talking about text. This is apparent when they employ programs which rely on a series of 'props' to build up a story. By rationalizing choice from among a variety of possible story 'paths', writers are required to focus on story structure, thereby talking explicitly about sequence and links among ideas.

The addition of animation facilities to programs will generate further new ways of composing and reading using videotext. Such facilities, however, need to be considered in terms of what they achieve in developing understanding of how meaning can be made by stretching thinking, and therefore learning, which would otherwise not be possible.

Databases

A principal function of databases, which are collections of files storing information, is to manage that information. Databases help children to sift through collected information and to search and sort it efficiently and quickly according to specific categories they can establish for themselves after negotiating their goals. Once sorted, information can be compared and contrasted, tabulated and graphed according to frequency of occurrence, or matched or rearranged to yield a variety of combinations, depending on the way criteria for sorting are established. Much of the activity required to use databases productively in classrooms occurs away from the computer itself, generating opportunities for teachers to teach children how to:

- establish the limits of a research project
- think through the nature of the information to be sought
- design appropriate data collection procedures (such as survey questionnaires and interview schedules)
- record and classify collected information
- organize that collected information according to an agreed classification system
- test hypotheses and make predictions
- make inferences and draw conclusions from the data.

One can readily see the application of database systems to extend the kinds of extracting and organizing information experiences that Morris referred to in Chapter 5, and to refine the procedures for categorizing information discussed by Weis and Stewart-Dore in Chapter 6.

What kinds of research projects might be served well by the use of databases? In her classroom, Newman (1986) and her students investigated their favourite poetry. After each student had shared five poems, it was clear that many dealt with similar issues and themes. It was suggested that the poetry could be grouped according to topics in order to compare each poet's treatment of them. Dividing into groups, students read the poems, decided collectively on the theme of each and placed it on a theme list. Lists were shared. Commonalities existed—food, animals, holidays, seasons, family, fear—but some poems defied classification: these formed a miscellaneous group.

To create a database file, however, more information than theme was required. Author, title and source were added. One group created a POEMS file and entered the categories decided upon. As time allowed, students took turns to enter information about different poems. They then sorted the data alphabetically for THEME, thus producing an ordered list of poems, which when printed out became a working file. To determine which authors and sources were recurring, these categories were also sorted alphabetically.

As Newman points out, nothing had been done thus far which couldn't have been done manually. However, when groups selected a theme for *comparison*, it was apparent that more information was required: categories such as poetic form, date written and imagery used had to be added.

The outcome of this activity was writing to compare poetry by reference to the sorted data. Some students chose to compare by theme; others by poet or form. Access to relevant information was facilitated by the database and an analysis of outcomes was added to the storage system. Newman suggests that this database could also be used to examine published poetry anthologies to determine popular themes and to compare these with those chosen by the class.

Database programs can assist in storing, sorting, classifying and analysing a host of 'real-life' information, thereby realizing the ambition of the Commonwealth Schools Commission's (1983, p. 27) recommendation that

> students should be introduced to learning experiences at the school in those areas where computers are being used in society.

This can be achieved by children exploring, through interview and questionnaire, people's attitudes about real-world issues, or by collecting and collating data that touches their lives. Examples might include studies of the nutritional value of food sold at the tuck-shop; the popularity of particular authors and titles amongst readers of different ages; the location, nature and effect of natural disasters; the 'value for money' of particular consumer items; the routes, discoveries and problems of various explorers; the measurement of area, length, width and weight of numerous objects, and so on. These topics fit naturally into regular curriculum activities but extend their application across supposed boundaries.

Database programs have been written to support learning and inquiry in particular subject areas. They are easy to use and encourage children to pose questions about the topic, to search the data and to hypothesize about, test and evaluate the data retrieved. Thus programs published by the Elizabeth Computing Centre such as *First Fleet: Convicts and Computers* and *Birds of the Antarctica*, and Know Ware's *The Explorers* and *The Bushrangers* databases have relevance in numerous curriculum areas. These latter programs enable children to plot courses on maps, recreate exploratory journeys on screen, compare routes, and learn through legends and ballads and historical maps. Prologic's *The Dream Machine*, suitable for older users, helps students to retrieve information about cars, to hypothesize about the impact of petrol prices and to recognize that statistical conclusions are tentative. Its application to Mathematics and Social Studies is clear. Thus we are witnessing the entry of educational database programs to assist content learning and thinking.

Adventure games and simulations

Thus far computers have been described as aids to writing, reading and thinking. A further application of computers in the classroom is that of generating co-operative activity and social interaction while integrating learning throughout curriculum areas, and this can be achieved by using adventure games and simulations. Nevertheless, no such program is of value on its own, and the critical factor in their effective use is how the teacher exploits the possibilities for wide-ranging creative activity beyond the computer itself.

Interactive computer programs promote problem-solving activity.

Children engage spontaneously in exploring real and imagined worlds through play, and adventure games and simulations capitalize on this natural behaviour. They further allow children to enter sets of conditions and environments, either fictitious or real, which would otherwise be impossible to create in school. As with reading books, time is required to enjoy, reflect on and share experiences, be they those of assuming the role of a character to interact with events, or working through choices, making decisions and using the imagination to find out information which will achieve a goal.

In the process children develop problem-solving strategies as they negotiate the program, knowing that mistakes can be put right. Interactive programs designed for classroom use also lend themselves to cross-curriculum activity.

One such program, *Flowers of Crystal*, has the potential, under teacher guidance, to generate a host of learning activities as children discover the need to think, plan, organize, pool ideas, and explore and test a range of possibilities. In doing so, they employ not only co-operative decision making, but also reading; writing stories, poems, captions for character portraits and mission statements; graphing to explain location; and interpreting grid references to locate a missing item.

Transported into the fantasy world of Planet Crystal, children might be stimulated to transform their experience of the adventure game into alternative media presentations. Such was the case with one class (Rutherford 1985), who created their own dramatic performance in two parts. To introduce the parent audience to their term's work and to familiarize them with the context, the children

- wrote an introduction to the characters and storyline
- created a cartoon tour of Planet Crystal
- presented an electronic program using Edfax pages for viewing on computer screens prior to the performance.

Preparation for the performance, in which hazards were negotiated to discover the last Crystal flower, hidden and protected by Rumala, involved children in

- negotiating the script
- writing poems and song lyrics
- designing and creating scenery, costumes and props
- improvising and rehearsing
- writing and publishing the program
- drafting and issuing letters of invitation.

Matson (1985) describes how his program, *Granny's Garden*, might be introduced. It was written specifically to generate cross-curriculum activity rather than to be used on its own. Activities in the first of eight weeks' interaction and discovery included:

- discussion about grandmothers and gardens
- drawing gardens
- imagining a garden adventure
- sharing orally told adventures
- enacting the oral story.

During the period in which children explored the adventure, they were involved in

- making a Magic Kingdom model
- drawing a cottage plan
- constructing dragon kites
- writing poems and songs
- measuring the playground
- creating magic spell recipes
- writing their own adventure stories.

Culminating activities involved the writing of a letter to the Magic Raven (who would send the children certificates). The children negotiated the letter contents which reviewed the range of activities they had engaged in, thereby re-visiting the Magic Kingdom and interpreting and responding to their experience.

Such possibilities for generating learning opportunities through computer technology are part and parcel of our emerging 'computer culture', especially as it applies to classroom contexts. Not only do we need to come to terms with the various applications of the computer in society, but we need also to learn how to use the computer to help children develop the skills and strategies that will enable them to solve problems through interactive and varied language use. Clearly computers have the potential to create the need to read, write and interpret real and imagined worlds.

Writing and reading the newspaper as a cultural artefact

A cultural artefact that frames, shapes and colours our world view and understanding is the newspaper. A versatile, authentic resource for teaching and learning, its potential for developing children's thinking and communicative competence is often not realized in schools. This is not to deny that many classes and schools regularly produce their own newspapers, or that teachers use the press to support teaching and learning in a range of curriculum areas. Unfortunately, however, many 'newspaper' activities designed as curriculum adjuncts are restricted to explanations of newspaper production and layout as 'special projects', or to the use of selected newspaper items for discussion or written response. While these activities have value, of themselves they do little to socialize children into cultural literacy. Children need many guided opportunities to explore how perceptions of social reality—historical, anthropological, psychological, scientific, ideological and so on—are created and shaped by diverse newspaper texts. Given such opportunities, they can develop awareness of and critical responsiveness to newspaper texts as an aspect of learning to write and read the world.

To guide children effectively, we must recognize (and teach them how to do so for themselves) the role that the popular press plays in mediating our acquisition of knowledge about, attitudes towards and understanding of events, customs, behaviours and issues that touch our everyday lives and those of others. Since the more technologically advanced our society becomes the more critical it is for people to be literate in order to control their lives, newspapers need to be regarded as significant artefacts that serve not only to mirror, but also to shape society.

One problem with using an authentic text such as the newspaper in the classroom, however, is that many teachers cannot get past thinking of it as primarily an adult text. Yet this is its major asset. Designed for quick, easy reading, with numerous graphics demonstrating the purposefulness of pictorial representation, and headings to signal possible meanings and to guide readers, the newspaper is a text which has its own attraction for children, allowing them to emulate adult behaviour. The instance quoted by Parkes in Chapter 2 testifies to how very young children readily immerse themselves in reading-like and conversational behaviour when they encounter the newspaper in natural use. As is the case with books and computers, it is through socially relevant experience with newspapers in a purposeful context that children learn how they work.

From experience and discussion of how newspapers are read procedurally, children can distinguish different purposes for reading and how these affect method and reading rate. As we know, many children come to school with understandings that newspapers are read selectively by surveying headlines to choose items to be read in detail; or by ignoring the news to turn to a preferred specialist section to update knowledge, check sporting results, identify television programs, or follow an episodic feature series. Others need to have these procedures modelled for them. Such procedural knowledge serves as an introduction to reading expository text with its topic specificity and organized sections signposted to guide the reader through the content. Useful comparisons can be made between the patterns of reading behaviour adopted for reading different kinds of text for varied purposes, and contrasts made with, for example, narrative text.

To capture children's interest in newspaper reading (particularly children whose cultural experience has not been shaped by home observation) the local press is often a stimulating starting point. This is because names and photographs of known people, places and events appear, thus fostering the understanding that newspapers chronicle happenings of a world in which the children themselves are active participants. Many local papers sponsor 'student reporter' columns, regularly featuring school activities.

Writing newspapers

There is no better way for children to learn how to interpret the many meanings of the press than by having them compose some to share with community members. Using actual publications as models, it is possible to generate questions so that children can probe the many facets of newspapers which work together to fashion meanings about the world. To compose their own newspaper facsimile, they need to grasp a number of explicit understandings. They must enquire, through systematic, planned observation and research, into:

- the characteristic features of, and rationale for newspaper organization
- the structure of different items—news reports, editorials, letters to the editor, reviews of the arts, entertainment guides, sports commentaries, feature articles, political cartoons and comic strips, advertisements, weather reports, regular columns
- the nature and kinds of mastheads, banner and other headlines, leads, bylines and captions
- how language is used to describe, record, report, quote, hypothesize, predict, confirm and verify, express opinion, argue, refute, and share knowledge, perceptions and understandings
- the visual effects of positioning items in particular places
- the ratio of news to features to advertising material to public service announcements and so on
- the role of photographs and other graphic data in highlighting, illustrating, demonstrating or commenting upon accompanying text.

Such research, when purposefully focused, allows children to gather information for analysis so that their text is appropriately informed. Those who have access to database computer programs can classify, categorize, label and store the information they have gathered for retrieval and analysis. It may be that the research data gathered by one class can be shared with another, with both collaborating to analyse and interpret results.

Of course, a database program merely facilitates such analytic thinking—it does not dictate or control it—and so these tasks can be completed without computer facilities by drawing up charts to record and display data, and to organize it so that it is both visible and accessible. The kinds of thinking about such data that are fostered include making inferences, comparing and contrasting information, and hypothesizing and drawing conclusions. The aim is to guide decisions about organizing children's personal or group news texts.

Roleplaying journalism

When asked, many primary children claim that they have written newspaper reports as class exercises. Undoubtedly, many do 'write newspaper reports' on researched topics, but rarely do these tasks demand anything but the most perfunctory of unguided writing episodes. Few children actually move through the disciplined observe-record-interpret-compose procedures that characterize professional journalists' time-governed writing. It is not suggested, however, that the hurly-burly rush of meeting deadlines be simulated in the primary classroom. Rather, teachers should examine what is involved in 'role playing a journalist' to compose and comprehend the *many* genres that comprise newspaper publication.

The principal role of a journalist or newswriter is, in Murray's (1985, p. 131) words, to 'probe, connect and affect what is happening—while it is happening'. We need to teach children how to uncover taken-for-granted everyday happenings, to connect ideas, and to shape meanings and actions through writing (and thereby, through critical reading). Thus we must charge them with investigating real issues and events which they are capable of influencing through their writing, rather than merely assign them report-writing tasks. To do so effectively, we must engage them in the processes by which news is *made*.

Journalists actively construct and interpret reality, by sifting systematically through interwoven experience to create ordered meaning. This involves collecting highly specific, accurate information, and selecting from that body of facts what is significant to report in 'truth' for a public audience. A journalist's principal tools are an interrogative mind coupled with a capacity for keen observation. Thus situations must be created in which it is natural for children to *need* to generate and pose questions to lay bare the heart of a matter of concern, so that they can genuinely observe to 'make news'.

What is required, however, is more than a written record of observed events and the people involved in them. Descriptions, procedures, causes and outcomes (or predicted likely effects), as well as opinions and attitudes, need to be filtered through observation and interview of both participants and observers. Children thus need to understand the nature of key questions to be asked about events, situations and interactions, either experienced directly or vicariously. Such questions might include the following:

- Who are the participants? What can we find out about them? Why and how are they involved?
- What is happening/the problem/the issue?
- Why is it happening/a problem/an issue?
- What are the background events and their context?
- Where is the event occurring? What is significant about its location?
- What might be the outcome of the event/happening/issue?
- What is the relationship between any/all of the events/participants?

Other questions will suggest themselves as children engage in self-chosen investigation of matters that affect them: be it the price of books or toys; the incidence of accidents in the vicinity of the school, home, or playground; the use of school facilities by community groups; the attitudes of people in the community (parents, workers, unemployed, elderly) towards social or political issues, and so on. In this way, the investigative work of professional journalists becomes classroom business as children negotiate the various meanings people around them attach to daily events.

Reading actual newspaper reports to examine the significance of these *kinds* of questions (and not to 'test comprehension') is an appropriate way of accumulating a variety of types of questions it is possible to ask about perceived reality. Children can also be shown how to challenge responses to questions by modelling and viewing recorded interviews that query the basis of assertions or statements of fact, thus building up a repertoire of questions that enable news to be 'made' through interpretation.

Some research will require critical reading of relevant material collected and discussed in class. The extraction and synthesis of ideas from others' writing demands that those strategies discussed in Chapters 5 and 6 be employed, thereby providing further opportunity for them to be exercised for self-sponsored purposes. Shared reading of items of interest to negotiate meaning and relevance, and to debate differences in interpretation, will arise naturally. No investigator of 'truth' can possibly read uncritically!

Preparing copy

The process of preparing actual newspaper copy is very similar to how children write in those classrooms where a process approach to its teaching has been adopted, except perhaps for topic assignment and who edits draft copy. In real life, journalists are assigned reporting tasks by the chief of staff and editor before embarking on research of the topic, issue or event. Through interviews and observation to record eye-witness accounts, they gather relevant information before drafting copy (usually on a word processor). After revision, they relay their report to the sub-editor, who edits it where necessary before creating a headline. The edited report is then sent to typesetters, compositors, photographers and pressmen for the last stages of publication. Finally, the journalist discusses the report and its possible effects on the public audience with colleagues and the chief of staff.

Thus, the recursive process of prewriting, drafting, critically reading, revising, editing, responding and publishing newspaper reports and articles matches that employed in many classrooms to compose extended text. Children who are used to such an approach will respond well to continuing projects that involve newspaper production. For those unused to text composition in this manner, newspaper production provides a real-world motive for employing and practising it. Apart from the modelling of the process of writing, newspaper copy preparation also demonstrates the co-operative negotiation of textual meaning which is at the core of integrated literacy programs and which also occurs in real-world situations. Children come to realize that adults can actually earn their living by researching, drafting, revising, editing and publishing every day.

Learning to structure text

Through writing, reading and discussion, we learn to shape reality and to create our own knowledge. It is through its various text genres that the press presents differing views of the world. Skilful journalists will employ language and text structure to influence and mould our thinking without us being aware of it. Indeed, we so take for granted the forms that newsmakers use that it sometimes comes as a surprise that we think about an issue in a particular way. We need therefore to teach children how to perceive these differences in ways of knowing and of interpreting the world, especially as we rarely have the chance to express *our* view in such a public forum. Perceiving such differences requires critical reading capacities, together with an insider's knowledge of how newswriters fashion the world. This is where writing to learn text structures assumes importance—not as an occasional venture into the world of the press, but as a regular part of a cultural literacy curriculum.

Mention has already been made of the variety of text structures or genres that are found in newspapers, and since these are unlike the more familiar structures of narratives and descriptions, children need to learn to discern how text organization serves to shape experience differently. Text types need to be modelled (perhaps by professional journalists rather than by teachers), analysed and practised intentionally in context, so that children develop understandings of their nature and purpose.

Probably the newspaper genres most frequently employed in classrooms are the 'news report', the 'editorial' and 'letters to the editor'. How many teachers, however, have engaged seriously in writing any one of them and for what purpose? It would seem that we all need to examine very carefully our familiarity with producing such texts before assigning children the task of doing so. A quick survey of obvious features demonstrates how variously the kaleidoscope of world views is shaped.

The news report

Traditionally using the 'inverted pyramid style', the writer reveals key information in an initial 'lead' paragraph, before elaborating. A lead captures succinctly the who, what, when, where, why and how of a happening. It is designed to allow readers to take possession of essential facts very quickly. Events recorded in a news report do not appear chronologically; less important, contextual information appears at the end, so that it can be edited out if space is at a premium. Most news reports (like some other newspaper genres) consist of one-sentence paragraphs, with few ever exceeding three sentences. Headlines signal the gist of a report, although banner headlines may sensationalize an aspect of an item to attract readers' attention, or signal an 'exclusive' report.

Editorials

Short argumentative essays, editorials vary in style. Some provide commentary on significant news events or issues and present a reasoned, defended point of view. Some appeal emotively for support for a cause, while others raise questions and issues for audience reflection and response.

Letters to the editor

These vary enormously in their language use and arrangement of ideas, but there are conventions to be followed. Those writing to initiate debate on an issue, or to express concern over a reported situation, usually state concisely the key point before providing reasons for holding a view. Those responding to letters already published are conventionally required to

(a) establish the letter's point of reference
(b) recapitulate the issue under discussion
(c) either confirm or refute something made public
(d) elaborate a personal viewpoint.

For publication, letter length is regulated. Thus effective 'letter-to-the-editor' writing requires the ability to state concisely a point of view, an explanation, an argument or a counter-argument.

Newspaper texts such as these exemplify the many diverse ways of knowing, and of mediating our thoughtful abstractions of social reality. Through them, and other kinds of text (be they oral, written, enacted, filmed or electronically generated ones), we develop, extend and shape our understandings of what is happening, what has happened and what may happen. It is through the publication of daily newspaper texts that we can witness the continuing construction and reconstruction of reality, and hence the creation of varied meanings and new knowledge.

Conclusion

According to Bowers (1984, p. 63), communicative competence, in its varied modes,

> involves the ability to problematise taken-for-granted experience as a necessary step in becoming culturally literate. Cultural literacy, in turn, leads to the level of understanding that enables one to call into question the underlying assumption that gives social experience its particular characteristics. This process enables the individual to actively participate in the reconstruction of social reality.

As teachers of children *meaning* to write and read their world, we need to challenge *our* assumptions about the nature of the experience by which we socialize children into the many literacies necessary to empower them to take charge of their future lives. We can do this by ensuring that the traditionally used cultural artefacts for literacy learning and teaching—books—are complemented by those which allow new meanings to be made every day.

References

Age, The (1985), Editorial, May 2, Melbourne.
Anderson, J. & Lovett, K. (eds) (1983), *Teaching Reading and Writing to Every Child*, Australian Reading Association, Adelaide.
Anderson, T. (1982), 'Assessing the impact of newspapers in education programs', Newspaper Advertising Bureau, New York.
Anstey, M.M. & Bull, G. (1986), 'Wreading is riting', *Praxis Network No. 1*, Centre for Research and Development of Curriculum, Darling Downs Institute of Advanced Education, Toowoomba.
Applebee, A.N. (1980), *A Study of Writing in the Secondary School*, National Council of Teachers of English, Urbana.
—— (1982), 'Writing and learning in school settings', *in* Nystrand, M. (ed.), *What Writers Know*, Academic Press, New York.
—— (1984), *Contexts for Learning to Write: Studies of Secondary School Instruction*, Ablex Publishing Corporation, Norwood.
Armbruster, B.B. & Brown, A.L. (1984), 'Learning from reading: the role of metacognition', *in* Anderson, R.C., Osborn, J. & Tierney, R.J. (eds), *Learning to Read in American Schools: Basal Readers and Content Texts*, Lawrence Erlbaum Associates, Hillsdale.
Baker, L. & Brown, A.L. (1984), 'Cognitive monitoring in reading', *in* Flood, J. (ed.), *Promoting Reading Comprehension*, International Reading Association, Newark.
Barnes, D. (1976), *From Communication to Curriculum*, Penguin Education, Harmondsworth.
Bartlett, B.J. (1985), 'Organisational structure: the key to improved comprehension and recall', *in* Unsworth, L. (ed.), *Reading: An Australian Perspective*, Nelson, Melbourne.
Beath, B. & Cox, D. (1981), *Reflections on Bali*, Addison-Wesley, Sydney.
Beevers, R. (1986), as reported by Dunn, R. in the *Daily Sun*, March 26, Brisbane.
Birds of the Antarctica, Elizabeth Computer Centre, Elizabeth.
Boomer, G. (1985), 'The newspaper and cultural literacy', Keynote Address given to the 2nd Pacific Area Newspapers in Education Conference, Sydney.
Bowers, C.A. (1984), *The Promise of Theory: Education and the Politics of Cultural Change*, Longman, New York.
Bransford, J.D. & Nitsch, K.E. (1978), 'Coming to understand things we could not previously understand', *in* Singer, H. & Ruddell, R.B. (eds) (1985), *Theoretical Models and Processes of Reading* (3rd edition), International Reading Association, Newark.
Brice-Heath, S. (1983), *Ways with Words: Language, Life and Work in Communities and Classrooms*, Cambridge University Press, Cambridge.
Britton, J., Burgess, T., Martin, N., McLeod, A. & Rosen, H. (1975), *The Development of Writing Abilities (11-18)*, Macmillan, London.
Brown, A.L. (1982), 'Learning how to learn from reading', *in* Langer, J.A. & Smith-Burke, M.T. (eds), *Reader Meets Author/Bridging the Gap*, International Reading Association, Newark.
——, Campione, J.C. & Day, J. (1981), 'Learning to learn: on training students to learn from text', *Educational Researcher*, vol. 10, no. 2.
——, Campione, J.C. & Day, J. (1984), 'Metacognition: the development of selective attention strategies for learning from text', *in* Singer, H. & Ruddell, R.B. (eds) (1985), *Theoretical Models and Processes of Reading* (3rd edition), International Reading Association, Newark.
Bullowa, M. (1979), 'Infants as conversational partners', *in* Myers, T. (ed.), *The Development of Conversation and Discourse*, Edinburgh University Press, Edinburgh.

Bunnett, A. (1985), *The Dream Machine*, Prologic, Abbotsford.
Caffee, R.C. & Curley, R. (1984), 'Structures of prose in content areas', in Flood, J. (ed.), *Understanding Reading Comprehension*, International Reading Association, Newark.
Calkins, L.M. (1983), *Lessons from a Child*, Heinemann Educational Books, Exeter.
Cambourne, B. (1984), 'Language learning and literacy', in Butler, A. & Turbill, J. (eds), *Towards a Reading-Writing Classroom*, Primary English Teaching Association, Rozelle.
—— (1985), 'Literacy matters: a personal view on the theme of the XIth Australian Reading Conference', in *Selected Key Papers of the 11th Australian Reading Conference*, Australian Reading Association, Brisbane.
Chandler, D. (1984), *Young Learners and the Microcomputer*, Open University Press, Milton Keynes.
Chapman, L.J. (1983), 'The reading development continuum: a framework for teaching reading', in Burnes, D., French, H. & Moore, M. (eds) (1985), *Literacy: Strategies and Perspectives*, Australian Reading Association, Adelaide.
Cheyney, A.B. (1971), *Teaching Reading Skills through the Newspaper*, International Reading Association, Newark.
Christie, F. (1984), 'The relationship of written genres to curriculum genres', a paper given at a conference on Language in Education, Brisbane.
—— (1985), 'Curriculum genres: towards a description of the construction of knowledge in schools', a paper given at a conference on Interaction of Spoken and Written Language in Educational Settings, Armidale.
Clay, M.M. (1979), *Reading: The Patterning of Complex Behaviour* (2nd edition), Heinemann Educational Books, Auckland.
Commonwealth Schools Commission (1980), *Schooling for 15 and 16 Year-Olds*, Canberra.
—— (1983), *Teaching, Learning and Computers*, Report of the National Advisory Committee on Computers in Schools, Canberra.
—— (1984), *Participation and Equity in Australian Schools: The Goal of Full-Secondary Education*, Canberra.
Connell, P. (1985), *Literacy and the Pre-School Child*, Queensland Pre-School Curriculum Project, Department of Education, Brisbane.
Courtney, J. (1984), 'Developing children's thinking skills through changes in teaching style', a paper presented to the annual meeting of the Australian Association for Research in Education, Perth.
Day, J.D. & Brown, A.L. (1980), 'Developmental trends in the use of summarization rules', a paper presented to the annual conference of the American Education Research Association, Boston.
Dixon, J. (1975), *Growth through English* (revised edition), Oxford University Press, London.
Downing, J. (1983), *Evaluation of the Consultancy Inservice Education Project on Reading to Learn at Bundaberg High School and Cooperating High Schools*, Queensland Inservice Education Committee, Brisbane.
Durkin, D. (1978), 'What classroom observations reveal about reading comprehension instruction', *Reading Research Quarterly*, vol. 14 (1978-79).
Ferreiro, E. & Teberosky, A. (1982), *Literacy before Schooling*, Heinemann Educational Books, New Hampshire.
First Fleet: Convicts and Computers, Elizabeth Computer Centre, Elizabeth.
Flower, L.S. & Hayes, J.R. (1980), 'The dynamics of composing: making plans and juggling constraints', in Gregg, L.W. & Steinberg, E.R. (eds), *Cognitive Processes in Writing*, Lawrence Erlbaum Associates, Hillsdale, N.J.
Gollman, A., Oberg, A. & Smith, F. (eds) (1984), *Awakening to Literacy*, Heinemann Educational Books, London.
Goodman, K.S. (1967), 'Reading: a psycholinguistic guessing game', in Singer, H. & Ruddell, R.B. (eds) (1976), *Theoretical Models and Processes of Reading* (2nd edition), International Reading Association, Newark.
—— & Goodman, Y. (1976), 'Learning to read is natural', a paper presented at the Conference on Theory and Practice of Beginning Reading Instructions, Pittsburgh.

—— & Goodman, Y. (1984), 'A whole language, comprehension centred reading program', Occasional Paper, Arizona Centre for Research and Development, Tuscon.
Goodman, Y. (1978), 'Kidwatching: an alternative to testing', *National Elementary School Principal*, vol. 57, no. 4.
—— & Altwerger, B. (1981), 'Print awareness in pre-school children: a study of the development of literacy in pre-school children', Occasional Paper no. 4, Program in Language and Literacy, College of Education, University of Arizona.
Halliday, M.A.K. (1975), *Learning How to Mean: Explorations in the Development of Language*, Edward Arnold, London.
—— (1985a), *An Introduction to Functional Grammar*, Edward Arnold, London.
—— (1985b), *Spoken and Written Language*, Deakin University Press, Geelong.
—— & Hasan, R. (1980), *Text and Context: Aspects of Language in a Social-Semiotic Perspective*, Sophia Linguistica VI, Sophia University Press, Tokyo.
Harste, J., Burke, C. & Woodward, V. (1981), *Children, their Language and World: The Pragmatics of Written Language Use and Learning*, NIE Final Report no. NIE-G-80-0121, Language Education Department, Bloomington.
——, Woodward, V. & Burke, C. (1984), *Language Stories and Literacy Lessons*, Heinemann Educational Books, New Hampshire.
Hasan, R. (1985), in Halliday, M.A.K. & Hasan, R., *Language, Context and Text: A Social-Semiotic Perspective*, Deakin University Press, Geelong.
Herber, H. (1970), *Teaching Reading in Content Areas*, Prentice-Hall, Englewood Cliffs.
Hornsby, D., Sukarno, D. & Parry, J. (1986), *Read On: A Conference Approach to Reading*, Martin Educational, Melbourne.
Houseman, A., *The Bushrangers Database*, Know Ware, Sydney.
——, *The Explorers Database*, Know Ware, Sydney.
Ives, D. (1986), 'Games can be learning adventures', *The Australian*, April 15.
Jagger, A. & Smith-Burke, M. (eds) (1985), *Observing the Language Learner*, International Reading Association, Newark.
Journal of Reading (1983) vol. 6, no. 1 (March), Australian Reading Association, Adelaide.
Kearsley, I., *Explorers*, Longman-Cheshire, Melbourne (in press).
Kennedy, N. (ed.) (1984), 'Newspapers: a media study', Provincial Newspapers (Qld), Nambour.
King, M.L. & Rentel, V.M. (1979), 'Toward a theory of early writing development', *Research in the Teaching of English*, vol. 13.
Kress, G. (1982), *Learning to Write*, Routledge and Kegan Paul, London.
Kruger, M. & Gaffney, L. (1985), *Teaching Foreign Language for Communication: Using Authentic Texts*, Queensland Department of Education, Brisbane.
Labov, W. & Waletzky, J. (1967), 'Narrative analysis: oral versions of personal experience', in Helm, J. (ed.), *Essays on the Verbal and Visual Arts: Proceedings of the 1966 Annual Spring Meeting of the American Ethnological Society*, University of Washington, Seattle.
Lawrence, J., Dodds, A., Volet, S. & Browne, M. (1984), 'The role of experience in problem solving and decision-making', a paper presented to the annual meeting of the Australian Association for Research in Education, Perth.
Lawson, V.K. (1984), *Read All About It! Tutor Adults with Daily Newspaper*, Literacy Volunteers of America, New York.
Lunzer, E. & Gardner, K. (eds) (1979), *The Effective Use of Reading*, Heinemann Educational Books for the Schools Council, London.
McGaw, B. & Lawrence, J. (1984), 'Developing expertise through higher education', *HERDSA News*, vol. 6, no. 3.
Marek, A. et al. (1984), 'A kid-watching guide: evaluation for whole language classrooms', Occasional Paper, Arizona Centre for Research and Development, Tuscon.
Martin, J.R. (1984), 'Language, register and genre', in the *Course Reader: Children Writing*, Deakin University Press, Geelong.
—— (1985), *Factual Writing: Exploring and Challenging Social Reality*, Deakin University Press, Geelong.
—— & Rothery, J. (1984), in Rothery, J., 'The development of genres: primary to junior secondary school', Study Guide Course in *Children Writing*, section 3, Deakin University Press, Geelong.

Martin, N., D'Arcy, P., Newton, B. & Parker, R. (1976), *Writing and Learning across the Curriculum 11-16*, Ward Lock Educational, London.

Matson, M. (1985), 'My teacher's a snarfer', *COM* 3.

Meyer, B.J.F. (1975), *The Organisation of Prose and its Effects on Memory*, North-Holland, Amsterdam.

Moore, T. & Roberts, W. (1984), 'Learning through databases', in McVitty, W. (ed.), *Children and Learning*, Primary English Teaching Association, Rozelle.

Morris, A. & Stewart-Dore, N. (1984), *Learning to Learn from Text*, Addison-Wesley, Sydney.

Murray, D.M. (1985), 'Newswriting', in Schwartz, M., *Writing for Many Roles*, Boynton/Cook Publishers, Upper Montclair.

Newman, J.M. (1986), 'Online: using a database in the classroom', *Language Arts*, vol. 63, no. 3.

Painter, C. (1984), *Into the Mother Tongue*, Frances Pinter, London.

—— (1985a), *Learning the Mother Tongue*, Deakin University Press, Geelong.

—— (1985b), 'The role of interaction in learning to speak and learning to write', to appear in Painter, C. & Martin, J.R. (eds), 'Writing to mean: teaching genres across the curriculum', Occasional Paper no. 9, Applied Linguistics Association of Australia.

Papert, S. (1986), in Ives, D., 'Directions for education: logo, Lego and life', *The Australian*, March 18.

Park, R. (1980), *Playing Beattie Bow*, Puffin, Melbourne.

Parker, R. & Davis, J. (eds) (1983), *Developing Literacy: Young Children's Use of Language*, International Reading Association, Delaware.

Parry, J. & Hornsby, D. (1985), *Write On: A Conference Approach to Writing*, Martin Educational, Melbourne.

Penton, R. (1985), *Evaluation of the ERICA (Effective Reading in Content Areas) Program at Massey High School, Auckland*, Department of Education, Auckland.

Quality of Education in Australia (1985), Report of the Review Committee, Australian Government Publishing Service, Canberra.

Robinson, H.A. (1975), *Teaching Reading and Study Strategies: Content Areas*, Allyn and Bacon, Boston.

Rutherford, R. (1985), 'Making a play of it', *Primary Teaching and Micros* (September).

Rumelhart, D.E. (1984), 'Understanding understanding', in Flood, J. (ed.), *Understanding Reading Comprehension*, International Reading Association, Newark.

Smith, F. (1971), *Understanding Reading*, Holt, Rinehart & Winston, New York.

Smith, J. (1985), 'Computers and literacy', in Burnes, D. & Page, G., *Insights and Strategies for Teaching Reading*, Harcourt Brace Jovanovich, Sydney.

Squire, J.R. (1983), 'Composing and comprehending: two sides of the same basic process', *Language Arts*, vol. 60, no. 5.

Stewart-Dore, N. (1985), 'Negotiating text: composing and computers', videotape script, Queensland Writing Project, Brisbane.

Thorpe-Clark, M. (1980), *Joey*, Addison-Wesley, Sydney.

Tierney, R.J. & Pearson, P.D. (1983), 'Toward a composing model of reading', *Language Arts*, vol. 60, no. 5.

Wagener, K. & Turley, P. (1985), *Auckland Star Teacher's Manual*, New Zealand News, Auckland.

Wardlow, E.M. (1985), *Effective Writing and Editing*, American Press Institute, Reston.

Watson, D. (1985), 'Whole language: definition and description', in *Selected Key Papers of the 11th Australian Reading Conference*, Australian Reading Association, Brisbane.

White, E.B. (1981), *Charlotte's Web*, Puffin, London.

Woods, C. (1983), 'Gutenburg, if you could see us now!', *Study of Society*, vol. 3, no. 14.

Wresch, W. (ed.) (1984), *The Computer in Composition Instruction*, National Council of Teachers of English, Urbana.

Index

Action research, 7
Analysing, 44, 58, 86, 90
Brainstorming, 43, 69, 72, 75, 77, 79
Categorising, *see* Classifying
Cause-effect relationships, 40
Charts, 79, 80, 90
   flow, 40, 43, 44, 46, 48, 51, 62, 78
   pie, 62
   retrieval, 40, 45, 49, 59, 60, 61, 62, 77
Class profile, 18
Classifying, 57, 69, 72, 85, 86, 90
Cloze exercises and tests, 64
Clustering, 40
Coherence, 2, 26, 32, 34, 85
Cohesion, 4-5, 69, 85
Comparison of ideas/information, 67, 69, 72, 77, 86, 90
Complication and resolution, 29
Composing and comprehending, relationship of, 2, 5-6, 35-38, 85
Comprehension, teaching of, 54
Computer
   adventure games, 84, 87-88
   culture, 84, 88
   databases, 83, 84, 85-87, 90
   functions, 84
   games, 14
   interactive programs, 88
   simulation games, 84, 87-88
   spreadsheet, 84
   technology, 83
   word processing, 84-85, 92
Conclusions, drawing of, 6, 8, 38, 47, 50, 54, 67, 72, 85, 90
Content Area Reading, 5, 53
Context, 9, 10
   curriculum, 81, 83
   for literacy, 82-83
   for reading, 54
   for unit of work, 45, 49
   for writing, 54, 79
   natural, 7, 12, 20
   of situation, 12, 25
Cultural artefacts, 7, 8, 83, 89, 94
Culture, 9, 23, 25, 81

Curriculum
   areas, 42, 86
   contexts, 81, 83
   differentiation, 31
Discourse pattern, 25
Discussion
   mixed ability, 65-66, 71
   small group, 65-66, 69, 71
Distinguishing main ideas, 57-58, 61, 69
ERICA, 5
Evaluation, 18, 19, 43, 44, 45, 46, 47, 48, 49, 50, 51, 70, 86
Experts vs novices, 65
Extracting information, 57, 62
Field notes, 8, 69
Freewriting, 69, 71, 73, 74, 76, 80
   recall, 72
Generalising, 6, 48, 57, 69, 72, 78
Generic
   choice, 26
   model, 25, 26, 30, 33, 34
   structure, 70
Genre, 4, 23, 24-34, 55, 79, 91, 92, 93; *see also* Text types
   definition of, 24-25
Graphic
   data, 90
   outline, 74, 75
   symbols, 84
Headings, 57, 60, 72, 74, 89, 90
Hierarchical relationships, 58, 73
Hypothesising, 6, 17, 19, 38, 44, 48, 50, 85, 86, 87, 90
Inferring, 6, 8, 38, 44, 48, 50, 54, 67, 69, 74, 77, 85, 90
Integration, 3, 6, 43, 51, 84, 87, 92
Intention, 36, 40, 42
Interaction, 4, 6, 11, 19, 36, 69, 83
   social, 9, 87
   writer/reader, 35-38, 40, 42
Journalist, role of, 91
Justifying thinking, 57, 69, 73, 74
Kidwatching, 4, 16-20
Knowledge
   application of, 38, 43, 44, 67

personal, 1, 78
prior, 8, 16, 19, 69, 72, 74, 75, 77
structuring of, 67, 68
Language
   analysis of use, 19
   as behaviour, 21
   as resource, 21
   concepts about, 11
   encounters, 10, 11
   functions of, 11
   nature of, 11, 21, 23
   registers, 55
   social significance of, 23
   user, 10, 11
Language learning
   as social phenomenon, 21-22
   conditions for, 10-11, 15-16
   oral, 9-11, 15
   processes, 3-4, 16-17
   written, 11-16
Learning
   control over, 6
   from text, 5
   in partnership, 11
   language, 22-23
   logs, 41, 42, 74, 79, 80
   processes, 43, 44, 64, 80
   responsibility for, 11, 15, 74
   to sign, 22
   to write, 23-24
Linguistic
   choice, 4, 7, 27, 70
   resource, 23
Literacy
   computer, 82, 84
   concepts, 55
   cultural, 8, 82-83, 84, 89, 92, 93
   graphical, 82
   in action, 12
   political, 82
   popular, 81
   program, 6, 40, 92
   social, 8
   socialisation into, 13-16, 19, 81, 89, 94
   teaching and learning, 1, 2, 3, 4, 53-54, 68, 69
   user, 13, 17, 19
Locating information, 74
Meaning
   as content, 23
   construction of, 35-36
   factual, 31
   intentions, 6, 9
   making of, 9, 10, 11, 19, 22, 23, 29, 81, 82
   negotiation of, 19, 84

personal, 1
potential, 12
reconstruction of, 35-36
sharing of, 9, 11
signing of, 14, 22, 82
system, 9
Metacognition, 6-7, 38
Modelling, 21, 52, 69, 89, 90, 91, 92
Models
   behavioural, 21, 34
   encyclopedic, 32
   expository, 30-31
   generic, 25, 26, 30, 33, 34
   learning from, 21-22
   linguistic, 22
Monitoring, 4, 7-8, 38
Negotiation, 51, 69, 77, 92
Newspapers, 13, 83, 89-93
Note-
   form, 60
   taking, 38, 44, 48, 57, 60, 66, 69
Observation, 7-8, 18
Organisational patterns, 60
Organising information, 35, 47, 57, 60-63, 77, 85, 86
   visually, 58-59, 62-63, 75-76, 90
Palm cards, 63
Peer tutors, 64-66
Pictorial chains, 78
Predicting, 49, 85, 90
Pre-writing, 46, 69, 78, 92
Print
   environmental, 8, 11, 14, 15
   social transactions with, 2
Problem solving, 40, 55, 67, 88
Process writing, 4, 54-55, 92
Processes
   material, 26, 27, 29, 33
   relational, 26, 32, 33
Questions
   inferential, 40
   posing, 86, 91
   predictive, 75
   self, 69, 74
Reading
   as developmental process, 53
   conferences, 19
   contexts, 55
   critical, 70, 80, 91, 92
   goals, 6
   interrelated with writing, 35-38
   linking ideas in, 63
   oral, 56, 57, 62
   purposes, 55, 89
   reflective, 74, 80
   schemes, 56

teaching of, 53, 54, 55-56
Records
   anecdotal, 18
   class, 18
   maintenance of, 7
Referential items, 32, 33, 63
Register, 55, 70, 79
   shock, 54
Risk taking, 11, 17, 18, 19, 72
Schema, 25
Schematic structure, 25, 27, 28, 29, 30, 32, 33
Signposts in text, 74, 89
Socialisation, 18, 21, 83
Sorting, 57, 58, 63, 85, 86
Structured overview, 72-73, 75, 77
Summarising, 57-60, 67, 69
   rules for, 60
Surveying text, 74, 89
Synthesising, 8, 43, 46, 78, 92
Text
   analysis of, 57, 60
   clues in, 64, 77
   composition, 4, 63, 84-85
   evaluation of, 6
   expansion of, 63
   nature and features of, 4-5, 54
   organization of, 5, 60, 67
   signposts in, 74, 89
   surveying, 74, 89
Text types, 4, 43, 52, 92
   artistic, 41, 42, 43, 44, 48
   autobiography, 69
   cause-effect, 5, 60, 62
   compare-contrast, 5, 58, 60, 61, 62
   description, 5, 48, 92
   diaries, 38, 41-42, 43, 44, 46
   editorials, 90, 93
   elaboration, 5, 60, 61, 93
   expository, 5, 29-30, 32-34, 41, 42, 44, 48, 62, 63, 67, 74, 89
   graphs, 38, 40, 42, 44, 48, 62, 88
   informational, 5, 79
   labelling, 26
   letters, 44, 88, 90, 93
   lists, 5, 18, 41, 48, 56-57, 60, 61, 69, 72, 86
   messages, 14, 17
   narrative, 28-29, 30, 41, 42, 43, 44, 48, 55, 62, 63, 74, 77, 88, 89, 92
   news report, 90, 93
   notes, 14, 15, 18, 41, 42
   observation-comment, 25-26
   personal, 41, 42
   plays, 41, 42, 51, 79, 88
   problem-solution, 5, 40, 60, 62
   procedural, 17, 40, 41, 42, 43, 44, 48
   recipes, 19
   recount, 27, 29, 30, 31
   report, 29-30, 32-33, 41, 42, 44, 47 48, 50, 52, 55
   utilitarian, 40
   variety of, 40, 47, 52, 55, 56, 66, 67, 68, 89
Thinking
   aloud, 65, 77
   critical, 44, 48
   development of, 55
   reading/writing as, 66
   reflective, 5, 6, 69, 74, 85, 87
Time line, 46, 62
Top-level structure, 5, 60, 77
Tree diagrams, 59, 60, 72
Whole language
   classroom, 17
   program, 18
Word maps, 69, 75-76, 77
Word processing, 84-85, 92
Writing
   across curriculum, 67
   as developmental process, 55
   contexts for, 54, 79
   creative, 23
   draft, 63, 69, 78, 92
   editing, 78, 92, 93
   influencing events through, 91
   interrelated with reading, 35-38
   revising, 78, 92
   to learn, 38-40
Written language principles, 12

Paula's Activities

She Tells us what happen at school every day start to make her events by using Her own writing.

Then she Reads again for many perposes